Staff Development

School Development and the Management of Change Series

Series Editors: Peter Holly and Geoff Southworth
Cambridge Institute of Education
Cambridge, CB2 2BX, UK

School Development and the Management of Change Series: 9

Staff Development

Howard Bradley

 The Falmer Press

(A member of the Taylor & Francis Group)
London • New York • Philadelphia

UK   The Falmer Press, 4 John St. London WC1N 2ET
USA The Falmer Press, Taylor & Francis Inc., 1900 Frost Road, Suite 101, Bristol, PA 19007

First published 1991

British Library Cataloguing in Publication Data
Bradley, Howard
  Staff development. — (School development and the
management of change series, 9).
  1. Great Britain. Schools. Personnel. Development
  I. Title
  371.00683

  ISBN 1-85000-827-2
  ISBN 1-85000-828-0 pbk

Library of Congress Cataloging-in-Publication Data
Bradley, Howard.
  Staff development/Howard Bradley.
    p. cm. — (School development and the management
of change; 9)
  Includes bibliographical references and index.
  ISBN 1-85000-827-2 — ISBN 1-85000-828-0 (pbk.)
  1. Teachers—In—service training—Great Britain. 2. Career
development—Great Britain. 3. Education—Great Britain—
Aims and objectives. I. Title. II. Series.
LB7131.B722 1991   90-25737
371.1′46′0941—dc20   CIP

Jacket design by Caroline Archer

Typeset in 11/13pt Bembo by
Graphicraft Typesetters Ltd., Hong Kong

Printed in Great Britain by Burgess Science Press, Basingstoke on paper which has a specified pH value on final paper manufacture of not less than 7.5 and is therefore 'acid free'.

Contents

Chapter 1

Staff Development and
School Development

What is Staff Development?

It made me look at myself professionally ... it's made me more articulate about what I do.

... from being very disillusioned, it's given me a lift towards the end of my career. I'm not burnt out as I thought I was; I have something to offer. I am going out on a high rather than a low.

... all the staff thought it made them think seriously about what they were doing in their teaching career. Not only about their actual teaching but about their present and future plans.

... this is the first time in fifteen years of teaching that someone has sat down with me for two hours and talked about me — my work, my successes, my problems and my future.

These statements, made by teachers who had just taken part for the first time in an appraisal scheme and recorded by Bradley *et al.* (1989), illustrate the value individuals place upon someone helping them to think about and develop their performance. The freshness and the surprise implicit and sometimes explicit in the comments bring home to us how seldom we have done this in the past. Staff development is, of course, much more than teacher appraisal but it has been subject to the same limitations. Where it has taken place it has often done so almost accidentally as a result of the persistence and determination of an individual teacher or through the vision of a particular headteacher. There have been few examples until recently of sustained, coherent and comprehensive programmes for staff development. Now, at a time of substantial pressure upon schools when teachers are reacting to changes in curriculum, changes in financial management and changes in accountability, the need for a well thought out system for staff development is becoming recognized as of central importance.

The statements with which this chapter began serve to remind us of the fundamental purposes of staff development. These are:

(i)   to make people feel valued in the job they do,

(ii)   to enable them to do this job well so that they receive the positive feedback essential for job satisfaction and for motivation,

(iii)   to help them to anticipate and prepare for changes in their work,

(iv)   to encourage them to derive excitement and satisfaction from their involvement in change, and

(v)   to make them feel willing and competent to contribute constructively to the development of the school.

These purposes allow a very wide variety of activities to contribute to staff development. Typically they fall into four categories, though any activity can contribute to more than one category and the evidence is that the outcomes are usually more positive if that is the case. The first two benefit teachers directly:

(i)   activities which improve teachers' performance in their present job,

(ii)   activities which enhance their prospects of career development.

The second pair look to the school's needs:

(iii)   activities which help the school to strengthen its present performance in areas where it feels deficient; for example, through staff changes it might find itself lacking expertise in a certain area of the curriculum,

(iv)   activities which help the school to meet future demands upon it.

Figure 1.1   The 'Road to Damascus' Model of Change

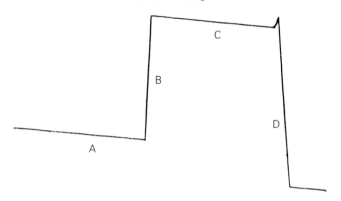

Different Perceptions of Staff Development

Most people subscribe to the idea that staff development is a good thing in the way that they might applaud the freedom of the press or the rule of law. When examined more closely, however, it rapidly becomes clear that the phrase means different things to different people.

One factor that divides people's attitudes to staff development is the view they take of change. One model of change is illustrated in Figure 1.1, sometimes called the 'Road to Damascus' model. It assumes that what we do gradually becomes less appropriate as the world outside the school changes. This declining relevance is represented by section A in the diagram. At some point the decline becomes unacceptable and a dramatic response is provoked, usually from outside the school, which forces a revolution in this aspect of its work (section B of Figure 1.1). Once the effects of the revolution have stabilized the gradual decline is resumed (section C), though from a higher starting point. Of course, the dramatic change sometimes backfires and the hoped-for quantum jump in performance turns out to be downwards rather than upwards (section D). This is a salutary experience for those involved but it is not uncharacteristic of this model of change.

Staff development on this model is concentrated in the periods of dramatic change. Its goal is to help staff come to terms with the need for revolution and with the demands which the change will make upon their teaching. Individual objectives and the methods by which they are approached will often be decided outside the school and the teachers are cast as the passive recipients of the process.

Figure 1.2 The 'Continuous Development' Model of Change

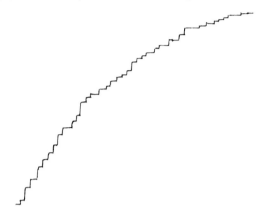

A different model of change is represented by Figure 1.2. This model abhors the 'great leap forward' of the previous model and instead adopts a policy of continuous improvement. It assumes that change takes place through a multitude of small steps, some of these forwards and some backwards. Through careful evaluation and monitoring, backward steps are identified very quickly and counter-measures are taken. On this model there should never be a dramatic collapse because teachers are always monitoring and always in control. This model relies heavily upon the quality of the monitoring process and it also makes substantial demands upon the professionalism of the teachers themselves.

For this model to be successful, staff development must enhance teachers' competence in the tasks of monitoring and decision-making. It must also give them skills of data collection so that they are aware of movements in the world outside and of the impact of their work upon those in their charge. It will be seen that these two models of change require quite different kinds of staff development.

Another factor which influences our perception of staff development is our view of the problem to be addressed and our role in its possible solution. For instance, an education minister who has introduced legislation for a change affecting all schools will necessarily take an instrumental view of staff development. It must enable teachers to deliver what the minister has promised. A group of teachers wondering how best to develop their school might take a quite different view. Individual teachers may have a different perception again, arising from their concern for their own career development. All these are legitimate positions, but they see different issues as important and staff development has to take different forms to satisfy them. Staff development for an infantryman may be very different from staff development for a dress designer. For an infantryman, desirable qualities might be obedience, stability, predictability and teamwork. Designers need to generate a constant flow of new ideas, to take risks and to exploit their individuality. The goals for staff development in these two cases are entirely different and one might expect that the staff development activities themselves would also differ substantially.

In some countries, views on the staff development of teachers have been coloured strongly by the debate about how a teacher's accountability should be expressed. This has led in some American states, for example, to goals for staff development which are targeted directly onto the achievement of a level of minimum acceptable competency. Deficiencies are identified, training in the appropriate competencies is provided and the teacher is required to reach the prescribed level. Such a model sits uneasily with views current elsewhere that the teacher as a professional determines the learning experience offered to students or pupils by observing them and listening to them, then deciding how to intervene in a way that helps them. Is a teacher's work akin to that of the production-line worker or is it more like that of a design-team member? The answer to that question is important because it determines whether staff development should aim to minimize the teacher's fallability or to maximize his or her creativity.

The arguments put forward in this book are based upon the proposition that for much of the time, the teacher's job of guiding pupils' learning is a creative and not a routine activity. They arise from a belief that change takes place most effectively in a school when the teachers feel they have control over the process. They also grow from an understanding that the development of a school and the development of its staff are related and mutually dependent.

How Can Staff Development be Put into Effective Practice?

If we are to progress beyond the present *ad hoc* arrangements for staff development, the benefits of which are also inevitably *ad hoc*, schools need to work out ways of helping individuals to identify accurately their own needs. This is no easy task for we are usually not too good at standing back from ourselves and looking at our work dispassionately. Our easily-expressed wants are not always our needs. The introduction of regular self-appraisal as part of the teacher appraisal process is of great benefit to us in identifying more clearly our individual needs. Certainly this was the evidence from the six LEAs (Local Education Authorities) involved in the national appraisal pilot study. It may be, however, that we can go beyond this. The use of a 'critical friend' to provide a second perspective of our work — talking with us at the planning stage, occasionally observing us teaching or sharing teaching with us, taking an active part in evaluating whether we have achieved the degree of success we planned — has been shown to be a very useful aid to self-evaluation. It is, however, much more than that, for it is a powerful staff development activity for both people; the 'critical friend' often confesses to learning as much as the teacher being helped.

Not only the individuals must identify their needs accurately; the school must do the same. If the school as a whole gets it wrong, then a lot of people are going to waste a lot of time attacking the wrong target. When a group of people has worked long and hard, only to discover it has had no effect, the demoralization that results is very hard to combat. There are now many systems available for whole-school review. The English GRIDS (McMahon *et al.*, 1984) system and the international IMTEC (Dalin and Rust, 1983) system have both been used successfully, and in response to Government initiatives many LEAs have introduced their own guidelines for producing school development plans. The School Development Plans Project refers in its documents to the process of establishing where the school now stands as 'audit'. Whatever the name given to it, the establishment of a clear view of the present position is vital to school development planning and to staff development planning. However, the crux of the matter lies in what follows the audit. Many schools, having produced an entirely competent review of their present situation, have found it much more difficult to assign relative priorities to the various lines of action which emerge from the review, or have been unable to do so without losing the commitment of groups of staff who have found their priorities not reflected in the final decision. Small schools seem to suffer less from this problem than large schools, where greater conflicts of interest often occur and where it is more difficult, if not impossible, for all staff to be involved in the process. The managing of the processes of assigning priority, constructing and implementing development plans, whether for school or staff development, will be revisited in a later chapter.

If school and individuals have been able to identify their needs accurately their next task is to reconcile the two. This too is unexplored territory for most schools. In the 'sixties and 'seventies staff development mostly meant attendance at courses and this was re-garded as very much a personal matter. The individual decided what course to attend and the expectation was that it would be the indi-vidual who would benefit. Headteachers and LEA officers saw it as their duty to support those who volunteered but the idea that the school or the LEA should seek some direct benefit would have been regarded as a strange one.

In recent years the pendulum has taken a considerable swing in the opposite direction. The immediate training needs of the school or the LEA have become the major determinants of how INSET funds will be used. This swing of the pendulum was strengthened in 1987 when the Department of Education and Science transferred funds, that were previously available through a national pooling system to enable teachers to study in Higher Education institutions, into the hands of LEAs, through the LEA Training Grants Scheme. This scheme, and the devolution of funds to schools which followed it, have had the beneficial effect of bringing resources closer to schools where the needs are identified. However, the simultaneous arrival of a host of curricular and other innovations on the doorstep of the school has had the effect of making school needs paramount, to the point of neglect of those of the individual. It has also meant that staff development, overwhelmed by problems of meeting the needs of today, has had little resource or time for considering the needs of tomorrow.

How then, can the needs of the individual and those of the school be reconciled? There is a good chance that, as individuals become used to taking part in the development of school priorities, they will begin to formulate their own needs in ways that complement the needs of the school and grow out of them. The teacher appraisal interview will for the first time allow a period of time when the individual's needs must be examined against those of the school. The targets agreed in the interview and the actions which follow will be important factors in achieving the reconciliation of the two. When targets are agreed in an appraisal interview, it will be essential that there is access where necessary to INSET funds. This, of course, is the real point at which the reconciliation takes place between the individual's needs and those of the school. If the appropriate funding arrangements cannot be made, then the point which has been reached is one of crisis, not of reconciliation.

In order to maintain the positive vision of staff development with which this chapter began it is clearly necessary to plan for positive outcomes and avoid the pitfalls which lead to reduced morale. A staff development policy is needed and it has to be one which is understood and in a real sense 'owned' by all concerned. The negotiation of staff development is a delicate and serious matter for the individuals concerned. They have to make concessions for the common good. The school in return must make some concessions to the needs of the individual.

Why is a policy statement needed? Because that statement will indicate the principles upon which any negotiation will be based. It will indicate where responsibilities lie for decisions and it will delineate boundaries. Perhaps most important, it will show how resources, of both money and time, will be committed to staff development. A policy without an indication of resource commitment is no policy, but simply an aspiration. A policy statement will also demonstrate the link between staff development and school development.

Most people accept that staff development and school development should go hand in hand. We know that:

* individuals find it hard to develop in static schools;
* schools are unable to develop without teachers changing what they do;
* if teachers do develop professionally, but individually, they may not be able to change their schools;
* sometimes when schools change, teachers do not change with them.

A good policy statement will set out practical ways in which staff development and school development will support each other, grow from each other and together enable the school to move forward effectively.

References

BRADLEY, H., BOLLINGTON, R., DADDS, M., HOPKINS, D., HOWARD, J., SOUTH-WORTH, G. and WEST, M. (1989) *Report on the Evaluation of the School Teacher Appraisal Pilot Study*, Cambridge, Cambridge Institute of Education.

DALIN, P. and RUST, V. (1983) *Can Schools Learn?* Windsor, NFER Nelson.

McMAHON, A., BOLAM, R., ABBOTT, R. and HOLLY, P. (1984) *Guidelines for Review and Internal Development in Schools*, York, Longman.

Chapter 2

The Needs of the Individual

Until the 1970s there had been little in the way of planned attention to the needs of the individual. Only with the emergence of the concept of INSET as a necessary part of the working life of every teacher did an interest develop in identifying the needs of the individual, so as to be able to plan the provision of INSET accordingly.

The first efforts at analyzing the needs of teachers led to some fairly naive models. These were either generalized from survey data or derived from an idealized notion of the career pattern of the typical teacher. One model read like Shakespeare's 'seven ages of man' speech as it pursued the teacher's development from professional infancy to professional senility. More sophisticated analysis soon showed, however, that the typical teacher is a figment of the imagination. Teachers in primary schools have very different needs from their secondary school colleagues. It will come as no surprise to learn that the perceived needs of women differ from those of men though the comparison is complex, being affected by the stage of the individual's career and by their mobility. Teachers' ages also influence their professional needs, but again not in a straightforward way. Finally, the constraints of geography — the position of the school or of the home — are critical factors in limiting the access of some teachers to activities intended for their support.

The understandings gained from these studies have been useful for planners and those who provide INSET activities in that they have demonstrated the complexity of the planning task and have demolished the idea of a common training pattern for all teachers. Instead, we are led to study the teacher as an individual and to plan a programme of activity matched closely to that person's perception of their needs. The change in emphasis is substantial — it means suiting activities to the needs of individuals rather than fitting individuals into

Cameo 2.1: *Jean*

Jean has been teaching for five years in Snowhill Infant School, her first appointment. At college she failed her final year's teaching practice and had to undergo a further practice. Her headteacher is absolutely astonished at this because Jean was from the beginning a very competent teacher and has developed into a superb one. Pupils blossom in her care, her classroom is a joy to visit and the quality of work on display is quite remarkable. The headteacher describes Jean as a perfectionist who is never satisfied with her own work.

In discussion, Jean's analysis of her own performance as a class teacher is strongly self-critical. She obviously doesn't see herself as a star. She is worried by the fact that the report arising from her recent appraisal interview does not reflect the concerns which she took into the interview about her own work. She feels she was railroaded into a more positive view by the head whom she described as 'a very strong character'.

The head admits that she set out to persuade Jean that she is an excellent teacher. She also hoped to persuade Jean that there is a lot she can offer to her colleagues in the way of guidance. Jean's reaction was to say all she wants to be is a better teacher. She avows that she has no ambitions to become a deputy head or head — 'all I want to do is to teach well'. After considerable pressure from the head she has agreed to become curriculum coordinator for science, and the targets arising from the appraisal interview were concerned with beginning to develop a system for supporting the other teachers.

activities. In reality, of course, the equation is more complicated than this. INSET activities take time to plan, so if providers waited until individual needs were identified before starting the planning process there would be considerable delay before the individual's needs were met. The process has to be one of continuing interaction between providers and teachers so that provision can closely match need. The basis for success remains, however, in a thorough understanding of individual needs. Their diversity is illustrated in the case studies which form the main part of this chapter.

Jean's case is far less unusual than it may seem. We can speculate about whether her unfortunate earlier experience of failure has persuaded her to concentrate her efforts on making sure that it never happens again. Is that why she backs away from new responsibilities and challenges? But it may be that she simply loves working with children and is determined to stick with that. Maybe she understands herself better than we understand her. How do we know that stretching her will be good for her? She clearly doesn't want to be in a position of risk and that is where our efforts might put her. However,

---

Cameo 2.2: *Alan*

Alan has recently returned to his school after a two-year secondment from a school to the LEA in which he acted as Advisory Teacher for TVEI (Technical and Vocational Education Initiative). Although he had been considering other posts he was quite content to return to the school because he had been very happy there. He said:

> I didn't know when I took this Advisory Teacher job whether I wanted to go into the advisory service or to think of deputy head jobs. I thought this would give me a chance to work out what I wanted to do. I know now the advisory service is not for me — I miss the school environment.

What surprised Alan was that no-one in the school has made any effort to capitalize on the skills he had gained as an Advisory Teacher.

> Nobody talked it over with me. It was just assumed that I'd go back and slot in as if I'd never been away ... I would have liked to get involved in the school INSET, I felt that after two years I had become quite good at INSET planning and delivery, but that's someone else's job and although I mentioned my interest to the head, nothing has come of it ... As I became more distant from those skills, I admit to feeling a loss of confidence. During the first term the euphoria of coming back into school carried me through and I felt elated. Now I'm beginning to think about the long term and to wonder where I'm going.

---

we also have to look to the future. If we do not extend Jean's horizon, what will she be like as a teacher in ten years' time?

The immediate points for action could be:

(i)   to raise Jean's image of herself. Praise is a useful weapon here but Jean is suspicious of praise. It may be better in her case to offer evidence of appreciation by others. If her new coordinator role works well, it could put her in the position of receiving appreciation regularly from colleagues;

(ii) to support her in her new role, ensuring she is trained for the new tasks to be done, helping her in the unfamiliar situation of guiding her colleagues and encouraging her to take the lead;

(iii) to seek to involve Jean in INSET activities outside the school which will broaden her professional horizon and encourage her to see her work in a context broader than her own classroom.

Alan's case is also fairly frequently encountered and is a classic example of prevention being better than cure. With hindsight, his headteacher recognized the frustration that Alan must have felt. He accepted some responsibility for the problem and felt there should have been a carefully structured plan for Alan's return which would have offered him scope for development as well as setting short- and long-term aims for him.

The opportunity to lead other teachers in curriculum development or planning or evaluation is an important part of staff development and when an individual has enjoyed such opportunities for some time, their sudden removal will inevitably lead to frustration unless they are replaced by another challenge which will offer satisfaction to the individual.

The introduction of the individual into planning teams is usually possible. Very often individuals who have been seconded return with administrative and executive skills which can be a boon to beleaguered senior management teams.

Advisory teachers often return to schools with experience of evaluation which is more comprehensive than that possessed by the rest of the staff. The pace of change being as great as it is, there is almost always a need for evaluation, and the evaluation of a school development doesn't necessarily require of the evaluator particular subject knowledge so that returning teachers can be used almost anywhere within the school, and not simply within their own subjects.

Another possibility is to create an alternative challenge, for example by encouraging the returning teacher to work for a higher degree, using the new skills to good purpose for the individual's personal development.

The example of Chris raises the important question of what to do when the individual's view of his needs differs from that of the school. Do we encourage Chris in his initiative, which is after all the first he has ever taken? Do we hope that getting involved in this course will perhaps widen his horizons? Alternatively, we could bring pressure to bear on him to get involved with those areas which clearly concern the Head of Science, but this could be a two-edged sword. Maybe, instead, we could bargain with him — a bit of what he wants and a bit of what we want. Cases like this bring out the advantages of regular appraisal interviews which allow both parties to put their cards on the table. Appraisal interviews always lead to a set of action points and in Chris' case it would be sensible to produce a planned progression with short-term and longer-term targets encompassing

Cameo 2.3:   *Chris*

Chris has been teaching for eight years in the same school. After graduating with an ordinary degree in physics he took a PGCE before applying to the school for a post as physics specialist. There were no other realistic candidates and the appointing committee were relieved to be able to make an appointment. Since then, as much on the strength of rarity value as anything else, Chris has received promotion within the school and appears to be satisfied with that. He has shown no signs of interest in moving to another school or in a headship of department. The family house in the country and village social life seem to offer all the satisfaction necessary.

On the teaching side, Chris does a more than adequate job, even if he doesn't make physics the most exciting of subjects. He spends a large part of the teaching week with the sixth form and upper school physics sets. Exam results are creditable and are a tribute to Chris's dedication to the subject. He has less liking for the lower age ranges, particularly when they have to be taught science rather than physics and in mixed ability groups.

Chris has never taken part in any INSET activities other than the occasional local meeting of the Association for Science Education. Stirred, perhaps, by discussion of the school development plan, Chris has indicated a wish to go on a one-term course on control technology as he feels his knowledge of electronics needs updating, particularly in terms of its applications, which are now very evident in sixth form syllabuses.

The request surprised the Head of Science and rather perturbed him. He has been trying to get Chris to take more interest in the younger and the less able classes. He would prefer Chris to get involved with INSET which would help to develop those areas of expertise. There are suitable courses about science for the less able and science in mixed ability groups. The Head of Science feels that Chris would also benefit from a series of visits to other schools. Chris gently evades these suggestions.

both Chris's goals and the school's. It ought to be possible to weave visits to other schools into this pattern. It would also be beneficial if ways could be found of getting Chris to work with other staff and perhaps even take responsibility for some particular aspect of school development. If this doesn't happen, we may find Chris looking more and more to village life for his stimuli and channelling more and more of his energies in that direction.

Sue is a very pleasant problem to have. She seems well able to plan her own life and to be very successful at it. Why not leave her alone to get on with it? In the hurly-burly of school life it is tempting to follow that line, but it ought to be resisted. Good teachers are entitled to support the same as any other. Sue is clearly cut out for headship but her path towards it can be eased by carefully planned support at the stage she has now reached. She now has to consolidate

---

Cameo 2.4: *Sue*

Sue has had a meteoric career. An Oxford graduate, she decided during her PGCE year that primary school teaching was what she wanted to do. She began work in a city-centre school. Her ability was soon recognized. It would have been hard not to do so, for in a very run-down school her classroom shone out like a beacon. She took her children out into the community as part of their work and started to bring members of the community into the school to share their expertise with the children.

Three years later she was offered and accepted a Grade B post for Science and Environmental Studies at a nearby school. Again she made an immediate impact and before long she became involved with development work throughout the city. A contribution to an HMI course brought her a stream of invitations to work with teachers throughout the north of England.

After another three very rewarding years, Sue decided she might begin to try for deputy headships. She was offered one at her very first attempt, in a large city on the other side of the Pennines. Six months into this new job, it looks like being another success story. Everybody likes her, she is excited by all the new challenges which face her in this very large primary school.

---

her management skills. She has to gain experience of working with governors and the community in a way that is different from their classroom involvement with her. She may need to extend her curricular experiences too. She can benefit from visits to other schools to explore their work. It would be very good for Sue and the school if she could become involved quickly in LEA developments in her new environment as she was in the old, though not necessarily in science.

Another good development activity for skilful people like Sue is to become involved in a research or development project which almost always stimulates participants because it takes them to the boundaries of their knowledge and puts them in a problem-solving situation. Maybe Sue ought to be considering a higher degree in Education.

Chapter 3

Establishing School Needs — School Self-Review

In most countries whose education systems are decentralized, interest has grown over the past decade in how schools with devolved powers of decision-making can respond systematically to change or can develop initiatives on a whole-school basis. A new vocabulary has developed, together with the inevitable acronyms without which no new movement seems able to survive. Different weightings and emphases are discernible, often related to the context in which the thinking developed, and the phraseology is very varied. Sometimes, however, it is the phraseology which confuses the reader and cloaks the essential simplicity of the ideas beneath.

The basic process is that of school development or school improvement. Within that process lie embedded various others; school-based review, self-evaluation, curriculum audit and school development plans to name but a few. Provided we can hold on to the idea that these latter processes are constituent parts of the broader whole, there is little difficulty in understanding their relationships. The problems have arisen because the groups developing these ideas started from different positions but all grew in the direction of school improvement. However, each group carried with it its own vocabulary, so that for some people 'school-based review' has grown to include under that title all the aspects we would associate with school improvement. For others, school development planning has grown in the same way. Within this chapter, school self-review will be examined in its narrower context as a method of identifying the school's needs. However, having adopted that position, let us remember that if needs are identified but nothing then happens as a result the expenditure of energy can hardly be justified. Review must lead to action, and to sustained action. Experience has shown that very often an approach to school improvement has been implemented apparently successfully by a school for one cycle, only for it then to falter because the process has not become the normal way of working for the school. Such reviews may lead to a 'Road to Damascus' conversion but they do not provide a strategy for continual improvement.

It is worth, at this point, summarizing the factors characteristic of good school self-review as they have appeared in research and development work so far:

(i)   school self-review is part of a continuing, cyclical process of review — decision — action — evaluation — review;

(ii)   this broader process is systematic, involving all who are concerned moving forward by negotiation and agreement. Its elements are those of planning, trial, evaluation and reinforcement or redirection;

(iii)   school self-review asks about where the school stands now, how well it is performing, where it wants to go in the future and how people feel about that;

(iv)   ownership of the process lies with the staff concerned. Data gathered are for the information of the staff and decisions on what to do as a result also rest with the staff;

(v)   the whole group needs to be involved. It is a shared activity;

(vi)   its purpose is primarily developmental, i.e. its goal is to improve the functioning of the school and the value its pupils get from it;

(vii)   even though its purpose is developmental, the fact of having carried out a regular review process places a school in a very strong position to demonstrate that it is carrying out its accountabilities.

School Self-Review as Part of a School Development Process

Almost all the school development projects place self-review within a continuing procedural cycle of activities. In its simplest form the cycle is composed of a series of questions. The cycle (illustrated in Figure 3.1) quoted by Holly *et al.* (1987) in their report of the DELTA Project (Dissemination arising from Evaluations of Local TRIST Activities) is typical.

The cycle begins with the general review activity 'What do we need to look at?' which is followed by a specific data-gathering ele-

Figure 3.1   The School Development Process (DELTA Project)

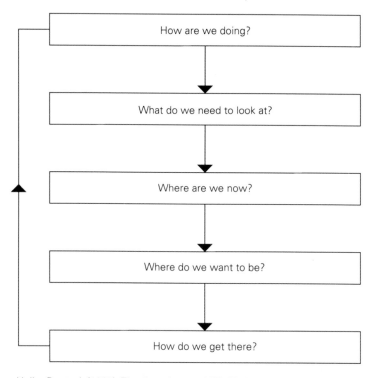

Source: Holly, P. *et al.* (1987) *The Experience of TRIST*, London, MSC.

ment 'Where are we now?' These two together identify the needs of the school and form the basis for the next stage which involves establishing priorities for dealing with the needs and taking decisions about 'Where do we want to be?' Having established the desired goals, decisions can be made about the ways in which those goals will be approached ('How do we get there?') and then the scene is set for the actual implementation of the agreed actions. The final part of the cycle is an evaluative one, 'How are we doing?', which helps the staff to see whether they have achieved the goals and are therefore able to move on to new issues, or whether they need to modify their strategies in order to satisfy their original goals.

Of course, in a continuing cyclical process it soon becomes point-less to talk about starting or final activities. Any activity in the cycle is informed and triggered by the preceding activity and in turn informs and triggers the succeeding activity, and, in theory at least, the process is self-sustaining. Because at each stage of the cycle, the teachers in the school have to discuss and answer the question appropriate to that stage, everyone knows where they are on the cycle and what the next task is. Holly *et al.* (1987) found three significant outcomes of staff involvement in this process. They reported as follows:

(i)   the involvement, in terms of both its scale and quality, encouraged staff development and the kind of cohesion and collaboration associated with the concept of 'collegiality';

(ii)   staff members tended to feel more positive about this style of change in school which we would call development as opposed to innovation;

(iii)   evaluation becomes the mechanism for transfer of ownership (of INSET and of the change process) to the schools. Co-ownership on the part of a school's staff is a most valuable outcome; it helps create an evaluative climate for INSET.

We shall return to these themes throughout this chapter, for they emerge repeatedly from each of the development projects and it is perhaps worth listing the main points here.

*   school self-review encourages staff development,
*   collaboration and collegiality are developed,
*   the style is developmental, rather than innovatory,
*   ownership of the process by its staff is important,
*   evaluation plays a central role.

The School Development Plans Project (Hargreaves *et al.*, 1989) suggests a very similar cycle (Figure 3.2) in 'Planning for School Development'. The Project describes four processes which together make up development planning:

(i)   *audit*, in which a school examines its present strengths and weaknesses;

(ii)   *construction*, during which a plan is agreed, establishing priorities and selecting targets;

(iii)   *implementation*, when the plan is put into action;

(iv)   *evaluation*, when what has been achieved is compared with what we intended.

In their report Hargreaves *et al.* report that teachers and headteachers feel there are eight main advantages of working in this way on development plans (DP):

Figure 3.2   *The School Development Process (SDP Project)*

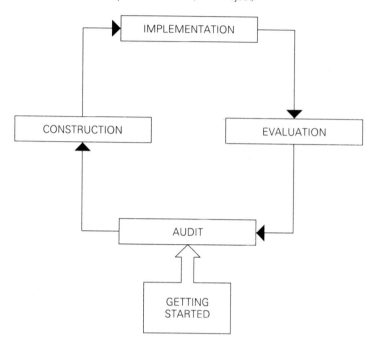

Source: Hargreaves, D. *et al.* (1989) *Planning for School Development*, London, HMSO.

1   A DP focuses attention on the aims of education, especially the learning and achievement, broadly defined, of all pupils.

2   A DP provides a comprehensive and coordinated approach to all aspects of planning, one which covers curriculum and assessment, teaching, management and organization, finance and resources.

3   The DP captures the long-term vision for the school within which manageable short-term goals are set. The priorities contained in the plan represent the school's translation of policy into its agenda for action.

4   A DP helps to relieve the stress on teachers caused by the pace of change. Teachers come to exercise greater control over change rather than feeling controlled by it.

5   The achievements of teachers in promoting innovation and change receive wider recognition, so that their confidence rises.

6   The quality of staff development improves. In-service training and appraisal help the school to work more effectively and

Figure 3.3 The School Development Process (GRIDS Project)

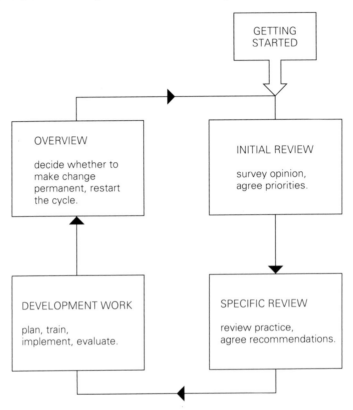

teachers to acquire new knowledge and skills as part of their professional development.

7 The partnership between the teaching staff and the governing body is strengthened.

8 The task of reporting on the work of the school is made easier.

Notice again how much importance is given to staff development, to ownership of the process by the staff and to making the process developmental.

Another example of the same kind of cycle is provided by the GRIDS Project (Guidelines for Review and Internal Development in Schools) (McMahon *et al.*, 1984). This is illustrated in Figure 3.3. Again there are two stages of needs identification. First, there is an initial broad-ranging review carried out through a staff opinion survey. This is followed by establishing priorities and carrying out a specific review in those areas. These then lead to conclusions and action in a similar way to other models, finishing with an evaluation stage and a return to the beginning of the cycle. In a report for the International School Improvement Project, Hopkins (1988) made the following commentary upon the GRIDS process:

1 SBR (School-based Review) requires an atmosphere of co-operative endeavour, not only within the schools which are expected to take on the process, but also in the educational system which supports the schools.
2 School autonomy cannot be total, and it is important to consider what parents, school governors and different levels of government would present as priority issues. In order to engender commitment for change, however, it is still the GRIDS team's view that the school staff must make the final decisions on priority for review and development.
3 The GRIDS team is still concerned at an apparent lack of rigour and objectivity in many review and development procedures. But to ask schools to produce clear criteria by which to judge their effectiveness is to set a complex task under the guise of apparent simplicity.
4 Schools which have worked through more than one cycle of GRIDS demonstrate a sequence growth. The first cycle serves to generate shared experiences, team-work, ownership of the process and confidence. Realistically it is in the second and subsequent cycles that one should expect increased rigour in procedures, application of clear criteria to present practices, greater openness to involving consultants and others, and a readiness to cope with external pressures for accountability.

As a contrast to the previous examples which illustrate a cyclical approach, it is worth examining the Institutional Development Programme (IDP) of IMTEC, the International Movement Towards Educational Change. This is a Norwegian educational foundation, the brainchild of Per Dalin who, with Val Rust, has developed the IDP and carried it into practice in many parts of the world. Although the individual steps in Dalin's (1988) model outlined in Figure 3.4 are similar to those in other models, IMTEC presents the process as much more of a linear progression from where the school is now to the desired future situation.

IMTEC's approach is also characterized by the belief that external consultancy has to be an integral part of the process, although Dalin

Figure 3.4   The School Development Plan (IMTEC)

PRESENT
SITUATION

1.   Recognition of need for change
2.   Establishing contract with consultant
3.   Diagnosis of school's strengths and weaknesses
4.   Planning, goal setting, problem solving
5.   Trying out ideas, receiving feedback
6.   Generalization and stabilization
7.   Completion and withdrawal

DESIRED
SITUATION

Source: Hopkins, D. (1988) *Doing School Based Review*, Leuven, ACCO.

makes it very clear that the role of the consultant is to provide motivation, expertise and support but that the responsibility for management of the process rests with the school, as does ownership of the changes which are introduced. These expectations emerge clearly in Dalin and Rust's (1983) list of the assumptions upon which the IMTEC method is based:

Assumption One: In spite of a much greater segmentation of organizational variables in educational institutions than exists in most industrial or commercial institutions, there remains a dynamic inter-dependence between most organizational variables.

Assumption Two: Because the organizational picture possessed by each member of an institution is both unique and limited, all members have an equal right to provide input data about the real nature of the organization and what it ought to become.

Assumption Three: An institutional renewal programme must be a collaborative effort involving as wide a scope of individuals in the institution as possible.

Assumption Four: Conflicts are normal organizational events and can be used constructively to facilitate the institutional development process.

Assumption Five: Institutional renewal usually requires some form of external support.

Assumption Six: Even though the consultation process of the

IDP is unavoidably not value-free, the consultants attempt to remain goal-free in terms of anticipated outcomes in the institutional renewal.

Assumption Seven: Sufficient degrees of freedom in environmental frames exist to tolerate school renewal efforts.

Assumption Eight: The effectiveness of the organization can be assessed only within a contextual framework.

Assumption Nine: Schools can learn.

There also emerges from these assumptions another characteristic of the IMTEC approach which may differ from the earlier examples, all of which lay strong emphases on consensuality. The IMTEC approach, both in its assumptions and in the survey instruments which it uses, emphasises individual perceptions of the present reality and of the future ideal. As a result, differences between individuals and groups are brought into the open and this is sometimes not easy to handle, hence the references to using conflict constructively in the assumptions. There are many who would argue that to have an expectation of difference and conflict is closer to reality, particularly in larger staffs, than to start with an expectation of consensus. There is some experience to suggest, however, that not all headteachers and staffs are able to use conflict positively and this can lead to difficulties for the continuation of the IMTEC process and for school development. Whether this is any worse than going ahead on a false assumption of consensus is a question the reader may care to ponder.

School Self-Review Instruments

Keeping the School under Review

During the late 1970s a number of LEAs in England and Wales were thinking about school self-review and in 1977 the Inner London Education Authority published *Keeping the School under Review* which became the model for many checklists produced by LEAs for the guidance of their schools. There were separate lists for primary and secondary schools and these were later revised and a special school checklist added.

Each checklist is composed of a series of questions which cover arrangements for learning, arrangements for care of the pupils, the school environment, links with the community, staff organization and management, together with some questions for each headteacher and teacher to answer. The lists form an excellent resource bank for those

Example 3.5   Keeping the School under Review, a sample section

Continuity

1 a What are the arrangements for achieving continuity in children's work other than the schemes of work?
b Who is responsible for the effectiveness of these arrangements?

2 Do teachers make their own continuing records of children's progress in intellectual, social, emotional, aesthetic and physical areas of development as a basis for completing the Authority's annual records?

3 Does the school have a common basic pattern for this recording?

4 To what extent are the school's current methods of recording successful:
   — in guiding a teacher's observation of children in the different areas of their development,
   — in identifying the needs of individual children,
   — in assembling information that is relevant to another school and for discussion with parents in the case of those for whom special educational provision may be required,
   — for that small number of children in primary schools for whom the Authority is maintaining statements of their special educational needs?

5 How is continuity promoted for individual children and in the different areas of the curriculum:
   — from home to school (including reference to playgroups, and so on),
   — from class to class,
   — from one school to the next (nursery to infants; infants to junior; junior to secondary)?

6 In transmitting information about children is reference made to apparatus or materials they may need or to particular teaching strategies which have proved successful?

7 What records are passed from stage to stage, for example:
   — longitudinal samples of children's work,
   — children's books,
   — annual records?

8 a What are the obstacles to achieving continuity?
b How are these obstacles being overcome?
c What further steps might be taken?

Source: the extract is reproduced by kind permission of Harcourt Brace Jovanovich Publishers, Limited. *Keeping the School under Review: the primary school.* (c) HBJ Limited. Originally published by the ILEA, 1982.

constructing their own self-review instruments. As an example, one section of the primary school checklist, that dealing with continuity, is reproduced in Example 3.5.

GRIDS

One of the problems of the LEA schemes of which 'Keeping the School under Review' is an example is that they were seen as externally imposed requirements linked with questions of accountability. In many cases this view was reinforced by an LEA requirement for the school to submit a report at the end of the process. Thus the work was often regarded as a chore to be done for the LEA rather than something that would have benefit for the staff themselves. In some LEAs it had not been foreseen that resources would be necessary to support schools wishing to proceed beyond the review to implementation of some decisions. This too reinforced the idea that the review's major purpose was not to help the school move forward.

The GRIDS project learned from these lessons as can be seen from the key principles outlined in the introduction to the booklets:

(a)   the aim is to achieve internal school development and not to produce a report for formal accountability purposes;

(b)   the main purpose is to move beyond the review stage into development for school improvement;

(c)   the staff of the school should be consulted and involved in the review process as much as possible;

(d)   decisions about what happens to any information or reports produced should rest with the teachers and others concerned;

(e)   the head and teachers should decide whether and how to involve the other groups in the school, e.g. pupils, parents, advisers, governors;

(f)   outsiders (e.g. external consultants) should be invited to provide help and advice when this seems appropriate;

(g)   the demands made on key resources like time, money and skilled personnel should be realistic and feasible for schools and LEAs.

The key step in the initial review is to administer a survey of staff opinion. That for primary schools is reproduced in Example 3.6. Section 1 is much shorter and simpler to complete than the ILEA document, and Section 2 carries staff into the process of ranking priorities. It is a necessary part of the process that the staff should decide how to analyze the data and who should do it on their behalf. A staff meeting is then called in order to identify areas to which priority for development should be given.

It is expected that the initial review in GRIDS will lead to a more specific review of the topic selected as being of top priority. Most small schools choose only one topic though in large schools it has proved possible to attempt more than one with separate teams of staff.

Example 3.6 GRIDS Initial Review

Standard questionnaire for canvassing staff opinion in primary schools

SECTION 1. Please indicate (by ticking in the appropriate column):

(i) the extent to which you feel the following aspects of the school would benefit from specific review and development

(ii) whether you think each aspect is an area of strength or weakness or is satisfactory

| Aspect of the school | Would benefit from specific review | | Strength | Satisfactory | Weakness |
| | (i) | | | (ii) | |
	YES	NO DON'T KNOW			
Teaching and learning					
Communication skills: 1 Speaking					
2 Listening					
3 Reading					
4 Writing					
5 English as a second language					
6 Mathematics					
7 Science/CDT					
8 Information technology and use of computers					
9 Creative and expressive arts					
10 Physical education					
11 Personal and social education					
12 National curriculum requirements					
13 Multicultural education					
14 Equal opportunities					
15 Provision for children with special educational needs					
16 Topic, thematic approaches					
17 Learning through first-hand experience					
18 Use of the environment					
19 Continuity of the learning process					
20 School ethos					
21 Extra-curricular activities					
22 Methods of grouping pupils					
23 Procedures for testing and assessment					
24 Pupil records, e.g. LEA record cards and internal systems					
25 Pupil reports					

Aspect of the school	(i) Would benefit from specific review			(ii)		
	YES	NO	DON'T KNOW	Strength	Satisfactory	Weakness
Staff and organization						
26 Staff development and in-service training arrangements						
27 Consultation and decision-making procedures						
28 Areas of curriculum responsibility						
29 Involvement of non-teaching staff						
30 Financial management						
31 Use of premises, materials and resources						
32 Care and maintenance of the school premises						
33 Communication with parents						
34 Parental involvement in the school						
35 Contacts with external pupil support agencies						
36 Relationships with school governors						
37 Links with receiving schools						
38 Links with pre-school agencies						
39 Links with special schools						
Please add any important topics not included above:						
40						
41						

SECTION 2. Bearing in mind that it may be as valuable to build on strengths as to improve areas of weakness, please select up to three aspects of school life from those listed above, including any added by you, and:

in column (i) write them in order of priority for specific review and development within available resources *over the next few months*

    (ii) explain what you mean by the topic and what the review should focus upon

Order of priority	(i) Aspect of school life	(ii) Explanation
1		
2		
3		

(Source: Abbott *et al.* (1988) *GRIDS Primary School Handbook*, York, Longman.) Reproduced with the kind permission of the National Curriculum Council.

Because this second review is specific it is much harder to prepare generalized material which would be effective in helping individual schools. GRIDS therefore offers no checklists but an action plan for the specific review. It has four steps:

    (i)   plan the specific review
- clarify the brief,
- identify key people,
- draw up a timetable.

    (ii)   establish what is current policy and practice
- seek documentary evidence,
- find out what really happens,
- report existing practice.

    (iii) decide how effective present practice is
- agree criteria and procedures for assessing existing practice,
- carry out procedures and apply the criteria,
- decide how effective current practice is.

    (iv) agree conclusions and recommendations
- identify main conclusions and recommendations for development,
- check with people likely to be affected,
- report the conclusions and recommendations.

It is at step (iii) that GRIDS leaves a great deal to be worked out in the school. The problems of establishing criteria for assessing the effectiveness of practice are quite substantial and, as will be explored in a later chapter dealing with the appraisal of teachers, the problems of establishing factual data about practice are even greater. There is a danger in all school self-reviews that, at this point in the process opinions, feelings, hopes and even prejudices fill the gaps between the facts. This danger has led the School Development Plans Project to pay particular attention to this stage.

School Development Plans Project — the School Audit

The School Development Plans Project is working in a very different climate from that existing when the GRIDS team was at work.

Schools now have to meet the requirements of the Education Reform Act. Their curricula must now satisfy the demands of the National Curriculum. They are required to make an annual curriculum return. What shape does school self-review take in that context? The SDP Project uses the term 'audit' to describe the process but it still places its purposes firmly in the area of development and growth:

* to clarify the state of the school and to identify strengths on which to build and weaknesses to be rectified,
* to provide a basis for selecting priorities for development.

The Project sees four important reference points for the audit:

(i)   the aims and values of the school, which really describe the fundamental purpose of the school so it is vital to ask how far they are being achieved;
(ii) the policies and initiatives of central government and the LEA, which extend or modify the school's own position;
(iii) recent reviews of the school by LEA or HM Inspectors, which add data and an external view of the school's practice;
(iv) the views of individuals and groups which add new perspectives, whether from within the school or from the community.

It suggests that two areas of a school's work

* curriculum provision and access,
* resources,

should be audited every year, but that other areas of its work should be visited in rotation. Because of the importance of the two obligatory areas, more guidance on their audit is given by the Project. On the curriculum side, it suggests:

* check that actual provision matches the planned curriculum and statutory requirements,
* locate gaps or overlap between subject areas,
* analyze the actual provision in terms of curricular objectives at the different key stages of the National Curriculum,
* assess whether teaching time has been well apportioned,

and on the resource side:

* establish how and why the school used its resources in the previous year,
* consider how to judge and ensure effective use of resources,
* decide how development planning can fashion resource usage, rather than the reverse.

References

ABBOTT, R., STEADMAN, S. and BIRCHENOUGH, M. (1988) *Guidelines for Review and Internal Development in Schools: primary school handbook*, York, Longman for Schools Council. (revision of McMAHON, A. *et al.*, 1984)

DALIN, P. and RUST, V. (1983) *Can Schools Learn?* Windsor, NFER Nelson.

DALIN, P. (1988) quoted in HOPKINS, D. (1988) *Doing School Based Review*, Leuven, ACCO for the Organization for Economic Cooperation and Development.

HARGREAVES, D., HOPKINS, D., LEASK, M., CONNOLLY, J. and ROBINSON, P. (1989) *Planning for School Development: advice to governors, headteachers and teachers*, London, HMSO.

HOLLY, P., JAMES, T., YOUNG, J. (1987) *The Experience of TRIST: practitioners' views of INSET and recommendations for the future*, London, Manpower Services Commission.

HOPKINS, D. (1988) *Doing School Based Review: instruments and guidelines*, Leuven, ACCO for the Organization for Economic Cooperation and Development.

ILEA (1982) *Keeping the School under Review: the primary school*, London, ILEA.

McMAHON, A., BOLAM, R., ABBOTT, R. and HOLLY, P. (1984) *Guidelines for Review and Internal Development in Schools*, York, Longman.

Chapter 4

Establishing Individual Needs — Teacher Appraisal

The Principles Underlying Appraisal

Whatever the quality of the school self-review, it is an inescapable fact that ultimately it is the way the teacher works with individual pupils which determines the quality of learning which takes place. This has led in the past decade to a growing interest in the appraisal of teachers.

A number of models from industry and commerce were available to early experimenters with appraisal. In 1985, Duncan Graham and his colleagues surveyed schemes in Britain and abroad, in education and in the business world. This work was published by Suffolk LEA (1985) under the title *Those Having Torches* at the time when interest in the introduction nationally of a scheme of appraisal was growing. Some examples of appraisal schemes appeared to have quite a lot to offer to British school systems, others had been disastrous failures even under their own conditions, and in others people seemed simply to be going through the motions in order to satisfy the minimum conditions of the scheme. Almost always the key to success lies in a clear expression of the purpose of the scheme by its initiators which is shared by its participants. Getting this climate right has proved to be vital and it forms a major part of the effort required to introduce a scheme of appraisal.

The reason why climate proves so vital is not hard to find. Appraisal comes closer to the individual teacher's performance, personal qualities and personal beliefs than any other professional activity. It is therefore seen by teachers as an extremely delicate operation, at least initially. It raises questions about the competence of the people who will take part in the process to carry out the intricate task of helping other adults analyze and improve their performance. It also requires some assurances about the confidentiality of information and records which are part of the appraisal process.

Exploration of schemes of appraisal for teachers in the United States demonstrated that appraisal introduced for purposes of accountability, that is to 'weed out' poor teachers or to make promotion or future pay dependent upon judgments made during the appraisal process, were seldom seen to be successful. At the same time in the United Kingdom many companies were moving away from schemes aiming to establish and maintain minimum competences through the application of sanctions or rewards. Instead they were beginning to concentrate on using appraisal to enhance the professional development of the individual and to see it as a way of ensuring that the support mechanisms available were appropriately matched to the individual's needs. The climate outside schools was therefore increasingly one which saw the purpose of appraisal as professional development and it was much easier to reach agreement between initiators and participants in the scheme if this were the purpose.

Unfortunately, the situation in English schools could hardly have been more difficult for the introduction of appraisal. Teachers, employers and the Government were in the midst of an industrial dispute over pay and conditions of service. Earlier DES (Department of Education and Science) documents and statements by Ministers had indicated the existence of a distinct accountability model in some Government circles and this had made teachers both sceptical and suspicious. Nevertheless, out of these unpromising conditions appeared the first signs of a way forward and they were incontrovertibly based around a professional development model of appraisal.

In June 1986 the Advisory Conciliation and Arbitration Service (ACAS) published the report of its working group on appraisal and training. As it turned out, it was the only agreement reached during the industrial dispute. The report covered agreed principles and some working arrangements for a pilot project.

The agreed principles are important, first because they demonstrate the professional development goals of the proposal and second because they became the fundamental principles of the pilot project, the School Teacher Appraisal Pilot Study (1987–89) and the National Framework for schoolteacher appraisal which followed it. In introducing the principles the ACAS document emphasized the continuity of the process:

> The Working Group understands appraisal not as a series of perfunctory periodic events, but as a continuous and systematic process intended to help individual teachers with their professional development and career planning, and to help

ensure that the in-service training and deployment of teachers matches the complementary needs of individual teachers and the schools.

This view is developed further by the National Framework (DES, 1990):

Appraisal shall be an integral part of the management and support of teachers, and not an isolated exercise.

In their final form in the National Framework, the principles are expressed as follows:

Appraisal schemes shall be designed to:
(i)   help teachers to identify ways of enhancing their professional skills and performance,
(ii)   assist in planning the in-service training and professional development of teachers individually and collectively,
(iii)   help individual teachers, their head teachers, governing bodies and local education authorities (where appropriate) to see where a new or modified assignment would help the professional development of individual teachers and improve their career prospects,
(iv)   identify the potential of teachers for career development, with the aim of helping them, where possible, through appropriate in-service training,
(v)   provide help to teachers having difficulties with their performance, through appropriate guidance, counselling and training,
(vi)   inform those responsible for providing references for teachers in relation to appointments,
(vii)   enhance the overall management of schools.

The ACAS Report emphasized the developmental nature of appraisal:

It will be seen that what the Working Group has in mind is a positive process, intended to raise the quality of education in schools by providing teachers with better job satisfaction, more appropriate in-service training and better planned career development based upon more informed decisions.

and this too is echoed in the National Framework:

> The aim of teacher appraisal shall be to improve the quality of education for pupils, through assisting teachers to realize their potential and to carry out their duties more effectively. It shall be a continuous and systematic process intended to help individual teachers with their professional development and career planning, and to help ensure that the in-service training and deployment of teachers matches the complementary needs of individual teachers and their schools.

At each stage in the development of plans for appraisal it has been made clear that the process should be related to the whole of a teacher's job and not simply to classroom performance and that all teachers should be trained for their part in appraisal, whether appraising or being appraised.

As a result of the ACAS Report, the School Teacher Appraisal Pilot Study was set up. It involved six LEAs — Croydon, Cumbria, Newcastle, Salford, Somerset and Suffolk. The project was funded by the DES and guided by a National Steering Group composed of teachers, employers and the DES. Each LEA had its own coordination team and the trials were coordinated nationally by a team from the National Development Centre for School Management directed by Ray Bolam. An independent evaluation of the Study was carried out by a team from the Cambridge Institute of Education directed by Howard Bradley. In all, nearly 2000 teachers and headteachers were appraised in about 150 schools representing all phases of school education. The findings of the Pilot Study were published by the DES on behalf of the National Steering Group in 1989, simultaneously with the Report of the Evaluation Team. In its Report (DES, 1989), the National Steering Group concludes that the pilot studies had provided clear evidence of a wide range of benefits for teachers and schools, including:

(i)   greater confidence and improved morale for individual teachers,

(ii)   better professional relations and communication within schools,

(iii) better planning and delivery of the curriculum,

(iv) wider participation in and better targeting of INSET,

(v)   better career planning,

(vi) better informed references.

Thus the Pilot Study had demonstrated that a climate could be built up in which an appraisal scheme based upon principles dedicated to professional development could work effectively. The hallmarks of such a scheme are that:

* first and foremost, it is concerned with helping the individual review his or her present performance and future concerns, agreeing the appropriate actions which should be taken as a consequence;
* it is a two-way process in that not only is the present and future performance of the individual reviewed but also re-viewed is the school's support for that individual. Typically, as a result of an appraisal there are action points for both individual and school;
* it is concerned with outcomes, not simply records in a file. Its aim is to develop every teacher and so to improve the teaching offered to pupils.

In introducing a scheme of appraisal, all the evidence suggests that it is vital to establish the correct climate. One step is to ensure that every teacher is aware of the characteristics of the scheme, particularly the hallmarks listed above, and feels comfortable with them. Equally, points of discomfort, perhaps based upon assumptions arising from an accountability model of appraisal, must be discussed and removed satisfactorily. Many schools found that a useful way to encourage confidence among their staff was to encourage pairs of teachers to observe each other teaching and then discuss what they had seen. This made teachers more comfortable with observation, one of the major worries in the minds of many, and at the same time gave them experience of the value of feedback and discussion. Finally, every effort must be made to ensure that all participants are clear about their part in the process, not only through training but also by providing materials which will guide and support both appraiser and appraisee while they are carrying out the various stages of the process.

The Main Elements of the Appraisal Process

After the creation of the appropriate climate and the commencement of a programme of training, the school must embark on its regular programme of appraisal. For each appraiser/appraisee pair this in-volves a planning meeting, data gathering activities, the appraisal

Figure 4.1   Components in the Appraisal Process: a biennial cycle

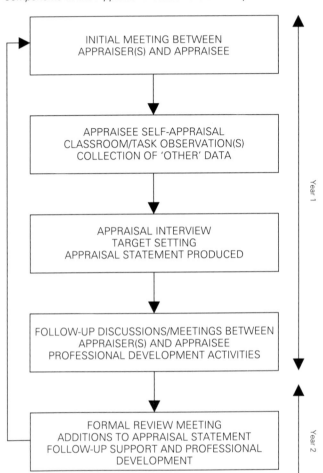

Source: Department of Education and Science (1990) *School Teacher Appraisal: the (draft) National Framework.* Mimeo. Reproduced with the kind permission of the Department of Education and Science.

interview itself, agreeing a written statement and a series of follow-up activities. The National Framework describes the process more fully in a diagram reproduced here as Figure 4.1.

The Initial Meeting

It became clear during the Pilot Study that the initial meeting (or sometimes meetings) is of far greater importance than was originally

Cameo 4.2: *Fred and Jenny*

Fred and Jenny snatched a few minutes after afternoon school one day in order to agree the pattern of Jenny's appraisal. They agreed it would be useful to get the process over quickly, while they both remembered their training and so that Fred could concentrate on the appraisal of Jenny before moving on to another of her colleagues. They agreed therefore to complete the data-gathering and interview within the next month.

Jenny said she didn't mind when Fred came to observe her teaching, in fact she would have preferred him just to pop in unannounced so that he would see her normal practice and not something specially staged for the occasion. However, they did agree two dates on different days of the week so that Fred could perhaps see different kinds of activity. In the event, Jenny did think rather more carefully than usual the night before about what she would do while under observation.

Fred and Jenny preferred not to concentrate on any particular aspect of Jenny's work in the classroom. Both felt that a better picture of Jenny's teaching would emerge if they didn't talk about it beforehand but instead left Fred to report what seemed to him to be important. They didn't discuss at the initial meeting what might take place in the interview. Both felt satisfied at the end of the meeting that they had 'got things moving'.

Fred carried out the observations as planned. The lessons went pretty well, Fred found it very difficult ignoring the children and eventually joined in the teaching. He gave Jenny brief feedback after the first observation but not after the second as the interview was the following day.

Jenny had done a self-appraisal as suggested in her training but she didn't share it with Fred and at the interview the things she had thought about didn't come up. Fred pursued an agenda for the interview which followed that suggested at his training. One or two of the items came as a surprise to Jenny, who wished she had been able to prepare for them, for example one about her role as a curriculum coordinator. Most of the discussion naturally centred around the classroom observation as that was their only common experience. Fred told Jenny how impressed he had been with her work. They spent a lot of time discussing three or four pupils and when it came to agreeing targets they were mostly related to some changed classroom arrangements to try to improve Jenny's control over them.

Afterwards Fred stressed how much he had learned about himself, through watching Jenny teach. Jenny said she had found the interview unthreatening and she was clearly pleased about that. She was also pleased that Fred had been so complimentary but she confessed that she had found the interview a little bit 'flat' — 'Was he being kind?' she asked afterwards. She also asked what was the purpose of the self-appraisal.

contemplated. It is not just the time when diaries are compared and dates fixed. It is the point at which the foci of the process are agreed between the two people concerned. Following on from that agreement it is possible to consider what data will be needed to support a useful discussion and how those data will be collected. Thus the initial meeting becomes the key to a purposeful appraisal. Comparison of Cameos 4.2 and 4.3 will make the point clear. Although they represent opposite extremes of the spectrum of appraisal processes observed during the Pilot Study, neither has been exaggerated in the writing.

Cameo 4.3:   *Pauline and Peter*

Pauline and Peter had done their training together, including a role-play exercise in which they practised interviewing skills. They felt this had given them confidence in each other and in the process. Perhaps because of this, they started off at the initial meeting by asking what they would spend their time on in the interview. Within the staff group they had agreed that everybody's appraisal would look at their contribution to continuity and progression within the school so that automatically went on the agenda. Pauline said she would like to discuss Peter's work as a curriculum coordinator as he has now spent two years in the job and Peter said he would like two items to be included — the way he dealt with the problems of children with learning difficulties and, secondly, plans for his own future career.

They agreed that those aims would form the agenda and that Peter's self-evaluation would concentrate on them. He suggested Pauline should look at it beforehand to save valuable time during the interview. They agreed that Pauline would look at a sample of pupils' work so as to generate some evidence that they could look at on the progression issue. They also agreed how she would spend her observation time, concentrating in part on a small group of pupils and in part on Peter himself. Finally, they agreed that Pauline should talk to other members of staff about the sort of support they received from Peter in his coordinator role.

Everything was done according to plan. The interview session took place soon after the observations and lasted for two hours. Peter was amazed that the time had gone so quickly — 'It was terrific,' he said afterwards, 'I don't think I've ever moved forward so far in one afternoon.' Pauline confessed to feeling exhilarated but exhausted. They had agreed one major target in each area for each of them, with a timescale attached to each. Pauline invited Peter to write the draft statement of the discussion with the understanding that she would make additions or alterations. None were necessary.

Self-appraisal

Self-appraisal is of central importance to most appraisals and many teachers remarked during the Pilot Study how refreshing it was to have reason to stand back and reflect on their practice.

A self-appraisal can be used at a number of different points in the appraisal process. Some use it right at the beginning to identify possible areas for discussion. Others use it after classroom observation as a way of making sense of what has taken place in the classroom. Others use it just before the interview, as a way of ordering their ideas.

There are as many different ways of carrying out self-appraisal as there are of using it and one person's meat is another's poison! Some people like to start with a blank sheet, writing in an unstructured way. Others prefer the discipline and the guidance of a list of prompting questions. Some use a job description or a list of key tasks. Those who have agreed on foci for an appraisal need a different kind of guidance list from that required for a more general approach. The list in Figure 4.4 is a good example of a general prompt list to encourage exploration of issues. Figure 4.5 shows a more detailed prompt list, developed by Newcastle LEA, all or parts of which could be useful in a more focused appraisal discussion.

Classroom Observation

For many teachers in the Pilot Study, classroom observation was the most significant part of the appraisal process. Before it took place it was the element which caused most nervousness but with experience of the process this was replaced with satisfaction at its value:

> I realized I was missing lots of things in the class. She was able to show I was achieving things.

> It enabled us to talk to each other about our work.

> We had to focus on specific things.

One group of teachers made the strong case that:

> Seeing other people's lessons is valuable in its own right — even without appraisal this would be worthy of consideration.

Figure 4.4   Self-appraisal Preparation Prompt Sheet

Prompting Questions

* Please respond to the following,

* Write in note form if you feel more comfortable in doing so.

(1) Do you feel your job description is relevant?

(2) Which aspects of your work do you feel especially pleased with?

(3) Which aspects of your job have not gone as well as you would have hoped?

(4) Are there any constraints or difficulties you are working under?

(5) In what ways would you hope to develop your experience and strengthen your expertise both in the coming year and in the long term?

Name _____

Date   _____

Source: Bollington, R. and Bradley, H.W. (1990) *Training for Appraisal: a set of distance learning materials*, Cambridge, Cambridge Institute of Education.

Certainly, in the Pilot Study there was agreement among the observers that it had been a very beneficial learning experience for them and this raises the question of why the benefits should be restricted to appraisers. In the context of staff development, there is a strong argument for setting up a system of peer observation within a school to which appraisers might have access as part of their data gathering.

A typical initial reaction to classroom observation was for appraiser and appraisee to agree that the observer should seek a general, overall impression — 'to drink in the atmosphere' as one appraisee put it. However, with experience the idea of a more specific focus has gained ground. People saw the general observation as satisfying any requirements for accountability and typically in this case the lessons observed were chosen for their representativeness and to show different aspects of the teacher's work. Those using more specific foci regarded classroom observation more as part of a process of professional development. In this case lessons were chosen for observation

Figure 4.5   Appraisee Prompt Sheet

APPRAISEE PROMPT SHEET

The following list of headings and statements indicates some of the important skills that all teachers, no matter what their responsibility, are required to possess.

The list is intended to help you to reflect on important aspects of your contribution as a member of staff.

Look at the statements under each heading and consider your ability/effectiveness in relation to each statement.

Please note: to make the list applicable to all staff group terms have been used

e.g.   people may mean colleagues, pupils, parents, etc.
group may mean class, committee, P.T.A., etc.
activities may mean a series of lessons, policy, initiatives, etc.

PLANNING	Experienced in/happy with	keeping my eye on this	need to spend more time on this	not relevant / of immediate concern
Perceiving your own class, department and school needs in the short term/long term.				
Setting and prioritising short term/long term aims and objectives.				
Collecting necessary information before making decisions.				
Drawing up a programme of activities to meet short term/long term aims and objectives.				
Using the most appropriate methods to meet the different needs of individuals.				
Generating new ideas, concepts and methods that improve situations.				
Making a conscientious effort to keep up to date with changes.				
Knowing your specialist area well enough to prepare strategies that are relevant.				

Figure 4.5 (Continued)

ORGANIZATIONAL SKILLS

	Experienced in/happy with	keeping my eye on this	need to spend more time on this	not relevant / of immediate concern
Adapting approaches to a programme of activities as necessary.				
Delegating tasks as appropriate.				
Managing time (e.g. meeting deadlines) and finance.				
Managing and using appropriate resources.				

FOLLOW UP SKILLS

	Experienced in/happy with	keeping my eye on this	need to spend more time on this	not relevant / of immediate concern
Monitoring and evaluating the effectiveness of a programme of activities.				
Systematically checking on standards of work produced.				
Insisting on high standards.				
Being prepared to accept the consequences of your decisions and taking action as necessary.				
Searching for methods to improve how things are done.				

COMMUNICATING SKILLS

Expressing ideas both orally and in writing in a clear and positive manner.

Giving clear guidelines of what is expected.

Liaising with outside agencies e.g. other subject areas, E.W.O.'s, parents, feeder schools.

Setting a good personal example as a model.

Providing information and advice to help others.

FOSTERING TEAMWORK

Being a member of/helping to foster an enthusiastic and productive group.

Involving people in decision making/identifying goals to gain their commitment.

Developing individuals to their full potential.

Developing self-discipline in a group and the ability to solve problems.

Successfully facing up to and dealing with conflict using the most appropriate method.

Accepting the responsibility to take initiatives/make decisions.

Figure 4.5 (Continued)

RELATIONSHIPS WITH PEOPLE

	Experienced in/happy with	keeping my eye on this	need to spend more time on this	not relevant / of immediate concern
Assessing your own capabilities.				
Seeing yourself as others do.				
Encouraging openness and honesty in expressing feelings between individuals.				
Recognizing how and when your behaviour adversely affects others.				
Adapting your own behaviour and attitude when they have a negative effect on working relationships.				
Maintaining good self-discipline even in the most difficult situations.				
Giving recognition whether in the form of praise or constructive criticism.				
Treating people fairly.				
Recognizing the needs and problems of others by sharing concern and understanding.				
Developing an atmosphere of trust and establishing a natural, comfortable and personal rapport.				

PROFESSIONAL DEVELOPMENT

Being aware of and involved in cross-curricular developments.

Gaining from and contributing to group work and courses.

Source: City of Newcastle Education Authority (1989) *STAFF Manual*. Newcastle: City of Newcastle Education Authority. Reproduced with the kind permission of the Education Authority.

because they illustrated the question or problem. They may well not be representative in that they might concentrate on a difficulty. This form of classroom observation calls for more confidence in the process on the part of the appraisee than more general observation. Those who did it that way maintain the benefits are considerably greater for the appraisee. At its best, the appraiser was seen to be performing a service for the appraisee, collecting and analyzing data in response to the appraisee's questions and helping the appraisee to make decisions as a result of the observation.

The success of observation depends heavily on the quality of the data collected and on the skills employed in feeding back to the observed teacher, which usually happened immediately or very soon after the observation.

Most teachers experience difficulties in observing. For many, the first problem was whether to participate in the lesson, responding to children and acting as a second teacher or whether to attempt to be a 'fly on the wall', a situation which they found unnatural. Participant observers tended to end up with little hard evidence they could share with their colleague, having usually been sucked into the lesson by the children and this is clearly a problem of this approach. Other observers were unaware of the variety of simple observation schedules which are available to them and most felt themselves in need of more training in their construction and use. They also found difficult the question of the criteria to be used. This was particularly the case when general observation had been attempted because participants found themselves carried directly into the very complex question of what constitutes good teaching. Those teachers who had chosen instead to concentrate on particular foci had fewer difficulties with criteria, because in setting up the issues to be observed some sorts of criteria were often constructed by the appraiser and appraisee as part of the discussion.

Remarking that classroom observation is a very complex activity, Bradley *et al.* (1989) suggested that its success depends on:

(a) the development of observation skills,
(b) following the preparation — observation — feedback phases of the clinical supervision model,
(c) selecting appropriately from the variety of approaches and procedures available,
(d) meeting the difficulty of establishing criteria and making judgments,

(e) ensuring that the record of the observation is objective and provides the basis for formative dialogue.

The feedback process is central to successful observation. Bollington and Bradley (1990) suggest that feedback works best if

* it is given within 24 hours of the observation;
* it is based on careful and systematic recording;
* it is based on factual data;
* the factual data are interpreted with reference to known and agreed criteria;
* the interpretation comes in the first instance from the teacher who has been observed;
* it is given as part of a two-way discussion;
* it leads to the development of strategies for building on what has been learnt.

Poor feedback, Bollington and Bradley say, is characterized by being rushed, judgmental, one-way and impressionistic.

Other Forms of Data-collecting

There is a danger that the natural interest in classroom observation may weight data-collection in its favour and indeed for some teachers their classroom activity is the major part of their job. Nevertheless, the National Framework makes it clear that appraisal should concern the whole of a teacher's job description and most teachers have pastoral duties and administrative or leadership roles relating to the curriculum or other areas of school life. For some, their job carries a substantial managerial role which may be as significant, or more so, than their teaching. This is particularly the case, of course, for head-teachers.

In all these cases the question arises as to what are appropriate data to collect and how best to collect them. How can you establish data about the way in which a curriculum coordinator, head of department or deputy head carries out work which is usually with other adults? One possibility lies in observing the activities, in a direct parallel with classroom observation. Observation can be general, in which case it is often called job shadowing, or it can be focused, in which case it is often called task observation. As with classroom observation, simple schedules are available which facilitate the observation of meetings or discussions and help towards useful analysis afterwards.

In some cases there is documentary material which can be collected and used as a basis for discussion — a sample of pupils' work, for example, or the schemes of work of a group of teachers.

While observation and collection of documentary evidence produce quite a lot of the detail which will help consideration of a teacher's role with respect to other adults, they leave a wide gap which can be filled only by referring to the other people concerned. Every teacher in a position of responsibility towards other teachers will want to know how those they work with perceive their performance. Collecting the data means consulting those people, either in direct conversation or through some form of questionnaire. Here, perhaps more than anywhere else in the process, it is vital that everyone in the school understands how the information will be treated and who will have access to it. One LEA has framed a set of ground rules which suggests that:

* what information is collected has to be agreed by appraiser and appraisee;
* the agreement has to cover who should be consulted, how and for what purpose;
* the agreement has to be reached at the initial meeting;
* information has to be collected, checked and fed back to the appraisee before the interview.

Figure 4.6 reproduces a neat analysis by Bollington, in Bollington and Bradley (1990), of the advantages and disadvantages of different forms of data gathering.

The National Steering Group recognized the sensitivity of this area of data collecting and as an appendix to its report it produced a code of practice for the collection of information, two sections of which are reproduced below:

General Principles
2   Information collection for the purpose of the appraisal of a teacher or headteacher should be designed to assist discussion in an appraisal interview having the purposes which have been agreed nationally.
3   Where it has been agreed that the appraisal should concentrate on specific aspects of the appraisee's job, information collection should likewise concentrate on those aspects.

Figure 4.6 *Approaches to Data Gathering — Pros and Cons*

APPROACH	PROS	CONS
TASK OBSERVATION	1. Useful way of focusing on and giving feedback on specific aspects of the teacher's work. 2. Can be used to give very specific, targetted support. 3. Relatively cost-effective as observation tends to be of finite, fairly short activities.	1. Takes observer away from his/her job. 2. Needs to be planned carefully to work. 3. Could lead to an artificial situation. 4. May be unfamiliar.
JOB SHADOWING	1. Useful to get the feel of someone's work. 2. Takes in everything over a half or whole day and so is unlikely to lead to an unrepresentative picture. 3. Gives a holistic view.	1. Time consuming. 2. Can be too unfocused and general to give specific feedback on areas for development.
COLLECTING VIEWS BY INTERVIEWS	1. Can get at data not otherwise available. 2. Can lead to valuable feedback. 3. Can be a useful way of testing an appraisee's perceptions.	1. Can be threatening. 2. Can result in interviewees suffering from a conflict of loyality. 3. Interviewees need careful briefing. 4. Time consuming. 5. Need for a fairly elaborate code of practice.
QUESTIONNAIRES	1. Useful quick way of getting a broad overview. 2. Relatively easy to administer.	1. Difficult to control how seriously they are taken or carefully they are filled in. 2. Not possible to follow-up initial responses as in an interview. 3. Things do not always come across as intended.

Source: Bollington, R. and Bradley, H.W. (1990) *Training for Appraisal: a set of distance learning materials*, Cambridge, Cambridge Institute of Education.

4 Appraisers should act with sensitivity to all concerned and should not exhibit any bias in collecting information.

5 Those giving information should not be put under any pressure save that of relevance and accuracy.

6 General comments should be supported by specific examples.

7 Interviews for the purpose of information collection should be held on a one-to-one basis.

8 Any information received anonymously should not be used.

9 Information which does not relate to the professional performance of a teacher or head teacher should not be sought or accepted.

10 Appraisees should not adopt an obstructive attitude to reasonable proposals for the collection of appropriate information.

11 Neither appraisers nor appraisees should act in any way that is likely to threaten the trust and confidence on both sides upon which successful appraisal depends.

Other guidance to the appraiser

18 The appraiser should agree with the appraisee at the initial meeting what information it would be appropriate to collect for the purpose of the appraisal, from what sources and by what methods.

19 When interviewing people providing information as part of an appraisal, the appraiser should explain the purpose of the interview and the way in which information will be treated.

20 Those giving information should be encouraged to make fair and considered comments which they are prepared to acknowledge and to substantiate if required.

21 Any written submissions should remain confidential to the author, the appraiser and the appraisee.

22 Those offering significantly critical comments should be asked to discuss them directly with the appraisee before they are used as appraisal information. (The substance of grievance or disciplinary proceedings should never be used in the appraisal process.)

23 Except where personal opinion is specifically sought (for example where an appraiser is attempting to gauge staff

reactions to a particular innovation), care should be taken to ensure that information is sought and presented in an objective way.

This code of practice has been adopted within the supplementary guidance issued with the National Framework.

The Appraisal Interview and Statement

The appraisal interview is the real innovation for many schools. Perhaps for the first time two people meet together to discuss the contribution of one to the school and the efforts of the other to support him or her. Participants in the Pilot Study saw it as a means of setting time aside to discuss jobs and careers and also to air views and points of concern. They found it the most rewarding part of the appraisal experience, reporting to the Evaluation team:

it's the first time in fifteen years' teaching that someone has talked to me for two hours about me, my job and my future.

it's quite exhausting, talking in a way that you don't normally do but also refreshing.

I came out very uplifted, highly delighted. I feel better, easier, know where I'm going and know I've got the head's backing.

Good interviews are usually born of good planning. In many schools there is evidence of a planned school-wide approach which led to a common understanding of what was involved. In one LEA the schools had:

* discussed the interview procedure in a staff meeting,
* agreed an agenda for appraiser and appraisee, used with appropriate modification for all staff,
* used common documents for preparation beforehand,
* agreed the way in which the statement would be written and agreed.

This common understanding of the procedure is a very important element of the success of interviews as is the thoroughness of the preparatory work. An agreed agenda allows both parties to prepare well and, if the data are shared beforehand, should ensure that there are no surprise turns to the discussion which might catch one or the other at a disadvantage.

Equally important as the preparation of the interview is the context in which it takes place. There must be privacy, comfort and freedom from interruption; none of them easy to guarantee in the hurly-burly of school life. Appraisees demanded a high level of commitment from their appraisers and were very intolerant of any interruptions or changes of schedule which might indicate that their appraisal was given a lower priority than other pressures on the appraiser.

The other important factors in the success of the interview are the personal qualities and skills of the appraiser. The role of the appraiser is to encourage the appraisee to explore the issues and seek his or her own conclusions, guided by the data which have been accumulated. The role is one of listening, aiding problem solving with the correct questioning techniques:

* open-ended questions to encourage exploration of possible alternatives,
* closed questions to establish facts or clarify details,
* reflective questions to explore feelings or philosophies.

The appraiser should summarize regularly and give a lead in drawing up targets and action points. This summarizing role is important in ensuring that each part of the discussion ends in a conclusion and leads to some further development. It is an important tool in ensuring that time is well-used as it enables the participants to conclude one discussion and move on to another. Summarizing also allows appraisers to check that their understanding of the discussion is what the appraisee intended.

Not all appraisers manage to be the paragons described in the role description prescribed above, but mercifully, Attila the Hun does not appear to ride roughshod through our schools, or at least not in appraisal interviews. There were occasions when the appraiser appeared to be saying 'why don't you do it like I do?' but most appraisees reported that their appraisers had been careful not to push their own opinions.

There were some occasions when problems were evaded. As one appraiser said, 'I trod warily. Next time I'll have more courage.' Such cases deserve sympathy. It is not easy to decide how far to push a disagreement in a small community where people have to continue working closely together afterwards. Nevertheless in other cases the nettle was grasped successfully and without rancour.

More usually, if appraisees were dissatisfied it was because they had been praised by their appraiser whereas their self-appraisal had been self-critical:

> It didn't document my concerns when I went into the interview. It is too positive. The head is a very strong character.

> The head went for all my good points. It was left for me to point to my failings.

Heads said:

> I had to drag out the successes.
> and
> We do praise one another, but not that often. It gave me a bit of opportunity to praise. People were pleased.

At the end of the interview one of the two participants, usually the appraiser, writes a statement which is an account of the discussion and the targets and action points which have been agreed. This statement is read and modified if desired by the second participant and finally agreed by both. Should there have been a disagreement during the discussion this can be recorded factually, with a clear explanation of both positions.

Experience shows it is important to write the statement very soon after the interview, before memories become clouded by other events.

Most LEAs have adopted very clear rules governing the access to appraisal statements, usually restricting it to the appraiser and the appraisee, the headteacher (if not the appraiser) and the Chief Education Officer of the LEA. Experience has shown that this desirable care for confidentiality needs to be relaxed in one respect in order to enable action to emerge from the targets and action points established during the interview. Very often such action points are for action by the school as well as the individual. Frequently they need introducing into the school's INSET plans and into the school development plan. The practice has therefore grown of appraiser and appraisee agreeing a separate note of targets for professional development and training which has a wider circulation.

Typically, according to Bradley *et al.* (1989) targets have fallen into three main categories:

(i)   classroom strategies, e.g. to make changes in the organization of the classroom, grouping pupils in a different way or developing a particular teaching strategy such as the introduction of a greater amount of computer based work;

(ii)   school performance, e.g. to carry out an additional responsibility such as taking charge of a cross-curricular initiative or taking on a coordination role;

(iii)   career development, e.g. to take on greater management responsibility within the school, or to go on a management course with a view to the next career move.

Most participants produced both long and short term targets and many found it valuable to place a clear timescale alongside each action. The longer term targets are often best achieved if they are accompanied by a sketch of the stages by which the target will be reached, including an indication of timing.

Experience has shown that target setting is most effective if the targets are:

*   quite specific, including within them who should be taking the various actions and what resources will be made available;
*   achievement orientated, indicating how progress towards them will be monitored and what will be the criteria for achieving the targets;
*   time related, so that there is an incentive to take action and also so that their realism can be checked in terms of the time available;
*   realistic and practical, not seeking to change the world;
*   not too many in number, less than six;
*   attainable but stretching, so that appraisees develop to the full extent of their capability.

It is often useful to report targets in an easily accessible format like that shown in Figure 4.7, which guides appraisers and appraisees into considering some of the success factors noted above.

Figure 4.7   Matrix for Reporting Targets

APPRAISAL TARGETS

Data of appraisal _____

Teacher _____

Appraiser _____

TARGETS	AGREED ACTION	STAGES IN THE ACTION	BY WHEN?	RESOURCES NEEDED	CRITERIA FOR SUCCESS OF ACTION
1					
2					
3					
4					
5					
6					

Reviews:

Date _____   Comments _____

Date _____   Comments _____

Date _____   Comments _____

Follow-up

Although there was evidence from the Pilot Study that there were substantial benefits for teachers and school which arose simply from engaging in the process culminating in the appraisal interview — the 'process' outcomes:

* incentive to reflect on one's work,
* time to discuss it with someone else,
* showing of appreciation and recognition,
* growth of confidence,
* enhancement of motivation,
* a clearer understanding of what is expected,
* feeling part of the school,

— it seems likely that these benefits would be limited to the short-term if there were no commitment in the scheme to follow-up. It is certainly hard to conceive of a scheme with the goal of professional development which does not give major importance to follow-up. It was to make this distinction that the ACAS report rejected the model of appraisal as

a series of perfunctory events

in favour of

a continuous and systematic process intended to help teachers with their professional development and career planning.

Any successful scheme therefore needs to present follow-up as an integral part of appraisal. Thus,

* targets should be clear, stretching for the individuals con-cerned but achievable, and have a timescale attached to them;
* each target should propose identified actions by identified people, so that there is a clear commitment to action;
* there should be follow-up meetings at which progress is re-viewed.

There is a danger, however, if integrating follow-up into the appraisal process isolates it from other aspects of the school's work. Follow-up to appraisal must also be integrated with the school's INSET policy and plans and its staff development plan. The school therefore needs

* a mechanism for fulfilling its part of the bargain for each appraisal,
* a system which harmonizes these individual bargains with school-wide policies and plans,
* a monitoring process to ensure that the system is working.

When emphasis is placed on follow-up in this way, evidence from the Pilot Study suggested that alongside the 'process' outcomes could be added a series of 'product' outcomes. For the individual the gains were twofold, first in skills development through experimenting with teaching or management style or through involvement in INSET, and second in career development through INSET on the one hand or change of role on the other. For schools, the benefits described included improved relationships, clarification of aims and increased knowledge and understanding among staff of the school's goals and practices.

Who Should Do It To Whom?

'Who should do it to whom?' is one of the questions which exercises many teachers contemplating the introduction of appraisal. The concerns which underlie the question sometimes derive from the model of appraisal the questioner has in mind. If the accountability model of appraisal were adopted in which the purpose of the process was to judge the teacher's performance against some national index of good teaching and grade the teacher accordingly, then we might expect teachers to prefer this to be done by their peers — 'the critical friend, someone who knows what the problems of the job are, someone I trust' — rather than by their immediate superior in a hierarchical structure — the 'line manager' in industrial parlance. However, when the model adopted is the professional development model, there is a good case for revising the argument. A cornerstone of the professional development approach to appraisal is that the process is two-way; the individual's performance is reviewed and so is the performance of the school in supporting the individual. It is essential therefore that the appraiser should be able to answer for the school's performance and also essential that the appraiser should be able to ensure that the school fulfils its part in meeting the targets. It is questionable whether the 'critical friend' can do this effectively, and before the end of the Pilot Study all the LEAs had adopted one form or another of the line management model. There is, of course, a major disadvantage to the line management model and this arises when there is a poor relationship between line manager and teacher. Some were for facing this problem head-on, arguing that where this is the case the school has a problem which is not restricted to appraisal and that the sooner such a problem is brought out into the open the better. Although this view carries the merits of openness and simplicity, most people baulked at the problems which might be introduced into delicately-balanced small communities in schools if it were insisted upon. Instead the line-management approach was adopted with an escape route — one LEA called it 'negative preference' — which allowed individuals to express a preference which would avoid undesirable confrontations.

There are other problems for the line manager approach to appraisal in some schools. Some teachers, especially in secondary schools where they might work in several departments, have several line managers. Others seem to have only tenuous links with a line manager — headteachers are perhaps the best illustration of this. Another problem is introduced because there is a limit on the number of appraisals any single person can carry out, usually thought to be four or five per year. This means that primary school headteachers, for example, often have to share their appraisal duties with their deputies and sometimes beyond, so a strict line manager approach is not always possible even where relationships are excellent. The necessity for ensuring that appraisers can fulfil their side of the bargain remains, however, and in such cases arrangements must be agreed to make certain that this is the case.

Use Of, and Access To, Appraisal Statements

The National Steering Group, in its Report, described appraisal statements as 'personnel documents of a particularly sensitive kind' and made the strong recommendation that access should be restricted to

(i)   appraisee and appraiser,
(ii) the headteacher,
(iii) the CEO (Chief Education Officer) and any LEA officer specifically designated by him or her,

with the exception that the separate note of targets for professional development and training might be forwarded to those responsible for planning training and development within the school and in the LEA.

It was expected that this restriction of access should be observed by the appraisee as well as the others, so the appraisee would not be free, for example, to use the statement as part of a job application.

The National Steering Group Report and the National Framework differed initially on how far the governing body of the school should have access to teachers' appraisal statements. The former felt a summary report would be sufficient but the latter suggested that the chair of governors should have access. The former now applies to teachers and the latter to head teachers. The two are agreed that the statements themselves should have a limited life, perhaps two appraisal cycles, and that all the other documents used during an appraisal should be destroyed immediately the appraisal statement is agreed.

Adherence to a set of rules such as this will resolve many concerns and remove possible sources of friction. It is perhaps worth now considering how the appraisal statement might be used positively by those who have access to it; the appraiser and appraisee, the headteacher and the CEO.

Appraiser and appraisee will use the statement:

(i)   in the follow-up review meetings, as a checklist for monitoring progress in achieving the targets;

(ii) as part of their preparation for the next cycle of appraisal, when it might suggest matters which ought to be on the agenda.

The headteacher will use the statement:

(i)   to assure himself or herself that the appraisal process has been carried out properly;

(ii) to monitor expressed needs in order to anticipate desirable changes in policy or shifts in the use of resources;

(iii) to seek issues which might need managerial action, for example disagreements or cases where, for one reason or another, appraiser and appraisee have not been able to achieve what they agreed.

The CEO or the CEO's designated officer will use statements:

(i)   to be assured that the school's appraisal system is working well;

(ii) to seek indications of INSET needs which might affect LEA or governor policy;

(iii)   to monitor how well individual needs are being integrated into the school's development plans.

Headteacher Appraisal

Good sense suggests that the principles and practices established for teachers should also apply to headteachers and this is generally the case. The points of difference are, typically:

(i)   It has been usual for headteachers to be appraised by a team of two appraisers: one, usually taking the leading role, a 'person with experience as a head relevant to current conditions in the place in which the appraisee works' (in the Pilot Study either a serving head or a seconded head); the other a professional officer of the LEA, to bring an LEA perspective on the head's performance and also to ensure that the LEA undertakes actions required of it in consequence of the targets.

(ii)   The data-collection phase is much more concerned with task observation and the collection of other informed opinion than with classroom observation. Because of the large number of people who might provide information — staff, governors, parents, LEA officers — it is vital that the agreed conventions for data collection are understood and adhered to. It has often been difficult to separate what is the headteacher's performance from the school's performance, sometimes because heads themselves take the view 'L'école, c'est moi'!

(iii)   The absence of an obvious line manager for heads within the LEA has made the role of the LEA officer appraiser quite a difficult one. In particular it has been difficult in some cases to ensure that appropriate actions are undertaken by the LEA. In addition, the growing role of the school's governors, as well as their control over resources, has emphasized in the case of headteachers the tension which the National Steering Group left unresolved between the managerial line stretching on the one hand from the head to the CEO and on the other from the head to the governing body. Who is now the head's line manager? Should the governing body have access to the appraisal statement? If that were the case, what additional safeguards would be necessary?

The appraisal of headteachers has been welcomed by heads very strongly, perhaps because their professional isolation makes them feel the need more urgently than teachers. It has emerged as being quite difficult to do well because of the difficulty of appraisers becoming familiar enough with the school and its practice, because of the time involved in data collection as well as its difficulty and because of the apparent difficulty in implementing targets which require action by the LEA.

Where Are We Now?

Once the National Framework is adopted within the conditions of service for teachers they will be required to take part in appraisal if their employers adopt a scheme in line with the National Framework. The National Framework, however, leaves considerable scope for the development and adoption of different models at LEA and school levels. A variety of practice is therefore likely so it may be worth summarizing what have been the lessons of the Pilot Study:

1 A professional development model of teacher appraisal works.
2 It demands considerable time and energy from those taking part.
3 Training is needed by both appraisers and appraisees and must encompass skills-coaching as well as awareness-raising. The time from training to implementation must be short.
4 The initial review discussion is of major importance in setting up a *purposeful* appraisal process — focus, data, criteria, agenda, targets.
5 Self-appraisal needs guidance.
6 Classroom observation makes people apprehensive, is well-regarded in retrospect, is a good learning experience for the observer and is often better if it is specific rather than general. The quality of the data from the observation gave some cause for concern.

7 Task observation and the collection of informed opinion was generally under–used in teacher appraisal and task observation was not well used in headteacher appraisal.

8 Interviews demand commitment and skill but were often very well done. There was no difficulty in agreeing a statement.

9 Targets need to be realistic and have a timescale attached to them.

10 A monitoring process is necessary to ensure that things happen as a result of appraisal.

11 Teachers were concerned that needs identified would not get a share of INSET funds.

One year later, the following additional points have emerged:

12 In some schools, appraisal has made a real impact on school development, staff cohesion and staff morale.

13 Evidence of success is much more available at primary than secondary levels.

14 Appraisal is now desperately needed to prevent individual needs being completely subordinated to school needs in the allocation of resources.

15 Classroom observation ought to serve other purposes such as developing the school development plan and may need to be separated from appraisal (but not lost). Perhaps it should be separately funded.

16 As so much is gained in classroom observation by the appraiser, is it sensible to restrict that to appraisers? There is much to be said for peer observation, with the appraiser having access to the data.

17 Appraisal of managerial responsibilities is still very much neglected at the data gathering stages of appraisal.

18 The role of the second appraiser, the CEO's representative, in headteacher appraisal is vital in bringing an LEA perspective to the appraisal and in ensuring an LEA commitment to the outcomes. It is not being done very well.

19 The role of governors in headteacher appraisal cannot be ignored. It may be good sense to separate governors as sources of data, governors' access to the outcomes of appraisal, and governors as appraisers, and decide policy on each separately.

References

ADVISORY CONCILIATION AND ARBITRATION SERVICE (1986) *Report of the Appraisal Training Working Group*, London, ACAS.

BOLLINGTON, R. and BRADLEY, H.W. (1990) *Training for Appraisal: a set of distance learning materials*, Cambridge, Cambridge Institute of Education.

BRADLEY, H., BOLLINGTON, R., DADDS, M., HOPKINS, D., HOWARD, J., SOUTH-WORTH, G. and WEST, M. (1989) *Report on the Evaluation of the School Teacher Appraisal Pilot Study*, Cambridge, Cambridge Institute of Education.

DEPARTMENT OF EDUCATION AND SCIENCE (1989) *School Teacher Appraisal: a National Framework*, Report of the National Steering Group on the School Teacher Appraisal Pilot Study, London, HMSO.

DEPARTMENT OF EDUCATION AND SCIENCE (1990) *School Teacher Appraisal: the National Framework*, Mimeo.

SUFFOLK EDUCATION DEPARTMENT (1985) *Those Having Torches*, Ipswich, Suffolk Education Department.

Chapter 5

Staff Development and School Management

The fundamental purpose of schools is to organize and develop the learning of their pupils. It follows that this must also be the fundamental purpose of any system of school management. Teachers enter into the equation because they are the school's most important resource. Not only are they the most expensive resource, as schools now embarked on local financial management have discovered, but they also have most direct impact on the pupils. No matter how far-sighted the National Curriculum might be, no matter how well organized the school is, the vital factor in whether a child learns or not is the teacher.

> If nothing happens in the classroom, curriculum plans are but wasted paper. (Department of Education and Science (1977) *Curriculum 11–16*)

When a child says something, writes something or does something it is the teacher who observes it, thinks about it and reacts to it in a way which either helps the child to consolidate its knowledge, or extends its thinking or develops its enthusiasm. That reaction is the fulcrum of learning. For teachers it is the high point of their professional skills. For the community, it is the reason why we send our children to schools rather than sit them in front of television screens. It is the interaction with teachers which matters.

In industry an expensive investment, particularly one which had the capacity to make or mar the product, would be the subject of constant monitoring and care. In education we are only just beginning to realize that teachers must be regarded as an expensive investment, and one that has to carry out a very sensitive and delicate process, probably for forty years. In the past there has been little systematic care for teachers, either for their individual professional well-being or for the way in which they mesh with the rest of the school system.

Succeeding chapters will examine methods of contributing in a systematic way to staff development. This chapter will examine the conditions in the school which are likely to maximize the success of a systematic approach to staff development.

Reaction to Change

The last few decades have been characterized by the increasing pace of change. It helps us to understand the process of change in education if we accept that change is basically unacceptable to most of humankind and that our generation is the first in which ideas come to practical fruition within a working lifetime. It took thousands of years for the invention of the wheel to affect the lifestyle of the common man, perhaps only with the coming of railways. The printing press, too, took two hundred years to affect everyone. Throughout the world in the nineteenth century we observed for the first time change within a lifetime, but it usually occurred through sons and daughters breaking away from the occupations and beliefs of their parents. Only in the twentieth century are we faced with changing ourselves, and on the whole we avoid it if we can. If this is the case, we must conclude that change has to be managed and that the implementation of change is a management problem as well as one for the individual.

In the 1970s there was considerable interest in the different attitudes adopted by people faced with change. Some of the ideas propounded then are quite useful in considering how to handle change and as a consequence how to choose appropriate modes of staff development. Such categorizations are often helpful at the stage of planning where, after brainstorming possible actions, a number of alternatives seem possible. One can then ask oneself how different categories of people might react to the different alternatives. A word of warning about their use is, however, necessary. Amusing as it may be to do, assigning one's colleagues into the categories described will almost certainly be counter-productive.

Doyle and Ponder (1977) described three different responses to change and characterized them as follows:

(i)   The 'rational adopters', the people who try to clarify the goals of the proposed innovation and the problems of achieving them. They deliberate on the available information and on different ways of solving problems. They try to choose rationally between alternatives and are keen to evaluate the outcomes of decisions.

(ii)   The 'stone-age obstructionists', the people who deliberately set themselves up as obstacles to change.

(iii) The 'pragmatic sceptics', people whose main concern is with immediate contingencies and consequences rather than with long term goals and outcomes. Their preference is for the real, concrete and practical rather than the abstract and theoretical. They are likely to describe their work in individual terms, emphasizing the uniqueness of each classroom and school.

Simple though it is, Doyle and Ponder's model helps us to understand why different proposals for handling innovation will emerge at a staff meeting. It also helps us to think through strategies for implementation to ensure that they meet the requirements of all three groups.

In a paper for the Organization for Economic Cooperation and Development concerned with the creativity of schools, Hoyle (1973) explored the concepts of restricted and extended professionality. He hypothesized the restricted professional as being characterized by:

a high level of classroom competence,
child-centredness (or sometimes subject-centredness),
a high degree of skill in understanding and handling children,
derives high satisfaction from personal relationships with pupils,
evaluates performance in terms of his own perceptions of changes
  in pupil behaviour and achievement,
attends short courses of a practical nature.

By comparison, according to Hoyle, the extended professional has the following characteristics:

classroom competence,
views work in a wider context,
participates in a wide range of professional activities,
  e.g. subject panels, teachers' centres, conferences,
has a concern to link theory and practice,
has a commitment to curriculum objectives and systematic evaluation.

In his paper Hoyle goes on to suggest that

The movement from restricted to extended professionality would be considerable in the case of many teachers. There is evidence that many teachers who have an intuitive approach to teaching would find the requirements of extended professionality too rationalistic for their taste. Similarly many teachers derive predominantly intrinsic interests from the activity of teaching and would not in the short term find satisfaction in the non-teaching activities which extended professionality involved.

If Hoyle's and Doyle and Ponder's hypotheses are correct, we have to face the conclusion that the management of any change must be a complex activity with a number of strategies for discussion and implementation related to target audiences with different philosophies and attitudes.

Characteristics of Successful Institutions

During the 1970s the focus of the search for understanding of professional development was upon individuals and how they change. In the 1980s the emphasis moved to the study of the institutional context in which the individuals work, with a view to understanding how that could be managed to maximize effectiveness in its performance and to make a positive contribution to the development of individuals.

The assumptions made in this work are that to achieve maximum effectiveness in performance, the institution must actively help the individual to develop, though at the same time staff development must serve the institution as well as the individual. The implication of these two statements is that the nearer to congruence we can bring the objectives of the individual and the objectives of the institution, the more likely we are to be successful.

What are the organizational features of a school, or indeed any other organization, which will make a positive contribution to professional development?

(i) Consistency of philosophy across all aspects of the organization. This point harks back to the need for congruence between the objectives of individuals and the institution. If different groups within the school have different philosophies and pursue different goals, the individual's development is often locked within one of those groups and he or she is unable to contribute at the whole-school level. Equally the school

itself must be consistent in all facets of its policy. Teachers will find it hard to be collaborative and collegial in one aspect of their work if everything else in the school is decided hierarchically. If responses to their initiatives are unpredictable, they will avoid disappointment by taking no initiatives.

(ii) Delegated responsibilities and a participatory form of decision-making. Several recent British researches have shown how this contributes to successful schools. Briault and Smith's (1980) study of schools suffering dramatically falling rolls showed how schools with active but democratic leadership and participative decision-making handled the situation more comfortably and reacted more effectively. Similar evidence emerges in the study by Rutter and colleagues (1979) of London schools, and in the HMI study *Ten Good Schools* (DES, 1977). In each case what was described was skilled and purposeful leadership, teamwork within the staff and consistent and recognized policies and processes, not an *ad hoc* laissez-faire free-for-all.

(iii) An expectation that things can be improved and a belief in evaluation. An interesting feature of successful institutions is that they are almost always comfortable with the idea of change. For them, it is the norm. Use of the word 'change' does not precipitate a shiver of apprehension, though very often they would prefer 'growth' to 'change' as a description of what they are about. Teachers see what they are doing now as a stage along the path of development and have an expectation that things can be further improved, that it is their job to identify what should be changed and to go ahead and do so. They believe in regular evaluation as the only means of identifying what has been successful and, in addition, what is not yet sufficiently satisfying and therefore a candidate for further change.

(iv) In Charles Handy's terms 'a bias for action'. Handy (1984), in a study of successful institutions, says they are characterized by what he calls 'a bias for action'.

* they put the emphasis on problem-finding, which Handy says is often more creative than problem-solving. The attitude is 'where is our next challenge', not 'Oh dear, look what's happened now';
* they put emphasis on control after the event, not before. As Handy puts it, 'try it and we'll see if it works' rather than 'ask permission before you do anything';

* they put emphasis on initiative. They encourage ideas, never kill one until it is tried out and never penalize failure if it is learned from. They have no fear of failure — 'to try is essential, to succeed is a bonus'.

(v) Trust that people will do a good job. Delegating responsibility means giving people the chance to do things their way. It means relinquishing some control, since their way might not be ours. Their accountability to us for their actions, of course, remains.

There are perhaps here the bare bones of a checklist for organizational health. It may seem to stretch a long way beyond staff development in its scope, but the evidence is beginning to build up that without good organizational health, effective staff development is impossible. Creating that situation of good organizational health is the task of school management.

References

BRIAULT, E. and SMITH, F. (1980) *Falling Rolls in Secondary Schools*, Windsor, National Foundation for Educational Research.

DEPARTMENT OF EDUCATION AND SCIENCE (1977) *Curriculum 11–16*, London, HMSO.

DEPARTMENT OF EDUCATION AND SCIENCE (1977) *Ten Good Schools*, London, HMSO.

DOYLE, W. and PONDER, G.A. (1977) 'The practicality ethic in teacher decision-making', *Interchange*, Vol. 8, No. 3, pp. 1–12.

HANDY, C. (1984) *Taken for Granted? Understanding Schools as Organizations*, York, Longman for Schools Council.

HOYLE, E. (1973) 'Strategies of curriculum change', in WATKINS, R. (Ed.) *In-service Training: structure and content*, London, Ward Lock.

RUTTER, M., MAUGHAN, B., MORTIMORE, P. and OUSTON, J. (1979) *Fifteen Thousand Hours: secondary schools and their effects on children*, London, Open Books.

Chapter 6

INSET Within the School's Everyday Practice

How Do People Learn?

Previous chapters have considered ways in which the needs of schools and the needs of individuals can be established and the last chapter discussed the climate which is necessary in schools to enable these to be met successfully.

This climate, characterized by

* consistency of philosophy,
* delegation and participation — 'many leaders' in Handy's words,
* searching for improvement,
* problem-finding, ideas and initiative,
* trust, 'freedom to do it your way',

is, at one and the same time, a goal for staff development and a prerequisite for it. It is a goal for staff development because people need to grow into working together in this way. It is a prerequisite because only when teachers have the challenge and the support which exists in that climate can they see the justification for the extra effort which is entailed in staff development and only then are they likely to receive the reinforcement which comes from a successful outcome of staff development.

What can schools do, therefore, within INSET which will both help to create that climate and capitalize upon it? It is worth stopping for a moment to remind ourselves what we know about how people learn. Although adults' strategies may be more sophisticated, there is no evidence to suggest that in the basic process adults are any different from children. Let us assume therefore that adults learn by comparing what they are hearing and seeing in the course of a current experience with knowledge, understanding and experience built up in the past.

When the current experience does not extend beyond previous experience, and can be explained satisfactorily on the basis of previous knowledge and concepts, there is a high degree of comfort but little learning takes place. Quite a bit of INSET in the past has been like this, with teachers choosing to attend courses on topics they enjoyed and in which they were usually very competent, rather than those subjects where they were unlikely to shine. This is a not unreasonable human reaction and we all do it, but it does limit the degree of development which takes place.

When the learner's current experience can be mostly explained on the basis of previously-established knowledge and concepts but when there are some puzzling contradictions, the learner is led first to question the contradictory evidence. If that is confirmed, the learner has to modify his or her existing framework of understanding in order to accommodate the new evidence. That is what we mean by learning. This was the process the providers of the INSET mentioned above thought they were utilizing, but very often their knowledge of the previous experience of participants and of their levels of development in that topic was so limited that they were unable to match them adequately. As a result participants either found they already knew it,

I enjoyed it, but it was mostly what I do already,

or it was beyond their present practice and unacceptable to them:

I don't know what sort of ivory tower he lives in but it wouldn't work in our school.

This last statement illustrates the learner's problems when the evidence of the current experience is vastly different from his or her previous experience. The learner is faced with a complete shake-up of some previous beliefs — a 'road to Damascus' conversion — or the alternative route of rejecting or rationalizing away the new evidence. Unfortunately, all too often rejection is the more acceptable course and no development takes place.

To have the best chance of success, it seems that INSET experiences should take participants beyond their present experience, but not too far, and should challenge their present understanding, but not too stridently.

It is worth remembering too that learning experiences are not restricted to those which come formally bound in an INSET cover. They happen all the time and for most teachers this means that most of their learning experiences are provided by the school, whether by design or not. So, if the conversation in the school staffroom never stretches the teacher professionally and never forces the teacher to question his or her assumptions, then the major influence on that teacher's learning is not being utilized. Similarly, if the culture in the school is very different from the ideas the teacher is struggling with, we know that in the end the teacher subsides into the school's value-system. We have two frequently-repeated examples of this. The first is that of new teachers, who come under very strong pressure to accept the norms of their school in their first job. Apart from the knowledge that they have to satisfy the school that they are fit to teach as part of the probation process, which is pressure enough to conform, it is quite usual for the school cynic to assure them

Forget all that new-fangled rubbish you learned in training. This is the real world.

The second example of a mismatch between teacher and colleagues emerges frequently after teachers have been seconded from a school, either for further study or into an advisory teacher role. On their return they often suffer the same kind of problems as the new teacher and are unable to put their newly-developed ideas into practice because of the scepticism of their colleagues. It has occurred so frequently that a phrase has been coined to describe it — the Re-entry Problem.

If the school is such an influential factor in teachers' development, we must face the question of how that influence can be used systematically for positive ends, rather than leaving it to drift along and being unsure of its impact.

Development Within Everyday Practice

What are the possibilities within the school's everyday life? What can be used to serve staff development purposes as well as its original purpose? What can be built into school life which will increase the openings for staff development? Some of the most useful possibilities are illustrated in the cameos which accompany this chapter. What is important is that these things out of which staff development might come should be used more deliberately. So that this outcome is surer, they are categorized below.

Observation

There are several sub-categories to observation. Cameo 6.1 describes one of them, pairing. Two colleagues who have a good relationship agree to observe specific aspects of each other's teaching. Almost always observer and observed both claim benefits from the process. One of the keys to the process lies in establishing a climate in which the observer acts as data-gatherer for the observed so that they can discuss it. Making judgments about the quality of the teaching is seldom productive in developmental terms, but analysis of the data and review of possible actions usually is. The period for feedback is as valuable as the observation and time needs to be set aside for it. This is the second key to success. The third lies in establishing a specific purpose for the observation, a particular question to be answered.

Visits to other schools present another opportunity for observation. Again the same keys are important — a clear, shared purpose, objective recording and open discussion. It may be more difficult to establish the right relationships during a short visit and there may be a need to make contact earlier in order to share the focus and purpose with the host teachers. It is often possible to multiply the gains from a visit by visiting as a group, thus increasing the amount of data that can be gathered and giving scope for more discussion upon returning to base.

Shared Planning and Teaching

This is under-rated as a contributor to professional development. Talking with a colleague while planning work, or reviewing what took place after the planned sessions both contribute to development. Sharing teaching is particularly good as it gives the teachers a shared experience to discuss. Videotaping a lesson and watching and discussing it together afterwards is another possibility. Evaluating children's work is another. In fact, any activity which encourages teachers to put up their ideas or their practice for discussion can be used purposefully for development. The discussion can be semi-informal and private to two individuals or it can be built formally into staff meetings or into staff seminars as in Cameo 6.2. Cameo 6.6 describes how four whole schools became engaged in this.

Specific Encouragement to Read

Cameo 6.3 is an example of how setting up a specific incentive to read can have benefits for the individual in terms of an increased knowledge base and wider experience of leading colleagues, as well as increasing colleagues' regard for each other's skills. There are obvious benefits for the school too in a wider distribution of knowledge and in keeping up-to-date with external events.

Providing a staff library is another way of encouraging reading, particularly if some kind of reviewing by staff is organized.

Involvement in Management and Decision-making

Management involves working with other adults; negotiating, persuading, arguing and taking decisions on their behalf. By its challenge, it demands a high level of response. It forces the individual to try to anticipate, to brainstorm, to plan and to evaluate.

All sorts of activities can be used for developmental activities in the area of management, not only with colleagues but also with parents and visitors to the school. All demand the delegation of powers to act, because only then do the management processes have teeth.

Leading Other Teachers

All the points made under management apply here too. The experiment and debate that is involved in writing materials, in leading discussion and in leading INSET are all strongly developmental for the teacher leader. Cameo 6.5 describes a particularly successful case.

Job Rotation

How do you deal with high-powered young curriculum coordinators who have made a tremendous impact on their curriculum areas and are now looking for other mountains to conquer? It may be a wrench

Cameo 6.1:   *Anne and Mary*

Anne and Mary taught parallel classes of 10-year-olds in a primary school. For a number of years they had collaborated in the preparation of topic work, sharing the task of accumulating materials and sometimes taking their classes on visits together or sharing a visitor to the school. They had never taken it further, however, by engaging in team teaching; indeed, they hadn't really ever discussed what happened in their classes when they used the material they had prepared, except in a very perfunctory way. It had never occurred to them that it might be interesting to watch each other teach and, had they wished to do so, they would have found it extraordinarily difficult to find the time to do so.

The opportunity arose for them when, in preparation for an appraisal scheme, their LEA proposed a scheme of paired observation and asked for volunteer schools. After a staff meeting, their school volunteered and Anne and Mary were paired. This time they planned to teach a topic in parallel and to observe each other three times. The first observation was a general one, to get a feel for the other's style. Anne was astonished and somewhat perturbed at how much more Mary's class seemed to achieve in that lesson than her class had. Wasn't she pushing them hard enough? Mary was aware of the difference but was unsure what was the cause. Could it be something to do with the way she had divided the work up into short bursts of activity for the children, between which she had guided the children gently towards conclusions, whereas Anne had given an introduction and some instructions after which she had left the children to move on at their own pace?

At the next observation they agreed to concentrate on what the children were doing to see if that gave them any clues. Attracted to the conversation one lunch break, the head suggested constructing a simple schedule to quantify the observation. Anne and Mary were glad they had done so because when they compared the two sessions they discovered that children in Anne's class had spent twice as long on off-task activities as had the other group. It wasn't that there was misbehaviour, children simply decided to take 'time out' to go to see what others were doing and there were quite a few cases of children moving round seeking inspiration for what to do next. Anne was still perturbed but at least she now had an idea what to do. She started experimenting with shaping the sessions so as to pace the children better. For the third observation they prepared together a lesson on Mary's pattern. It went well for Anne and to her relief the schedule this time showed no difference between the two groups. She was very glad that the solution turned out to be so simple but she remarked afterwards that the difference must have been there for years and she had never known.

Cameo 6.2: *Tony*

The head of Tony's school had, upon his appointment, begun a series of termly seminars for the staff in which he asked everyone to read a short article circulated beforehand about which there would be a hour's discussion. Tony was sceptical. He really went to the first couple to see if they would fall flat. He was convinced most of the staff, like him, never did any educational reading except the back pages of the *Times Educational Supplement*! He wasn't intending to make much of a contribution but the second session was controversial and got quite heated. Tony couldn't resist putting his oar in. Five minutes later he rather wished he hadn't as his contribution was dissected and refuted by three of his colleagues. Despite that, he found himself feeling quite elated at the end. They had thrashed their way through it and had finally reached agreement. Not only that, they had also decided how as a staff they would handle the issue in school.

Determined not to be caught again, Tony did a bit of reading before the next seminar. He found himself looking forward to it and once again he enjoyed it. Not only that, he found out a lot about his colleagues. Funny how you could work alongside them for years and not really know what they believed.

Later that year, the National Curriculum documents started flowing towards schools. The head said 'Shall we have seminars on them?' The staff were ready.

Cameo 6.3: *Rebecca*

The head caught Becky on the way into school one day and said that she was growing concerned about the flood of papers, reports, guidance material and so on which was nowadays addressed to schools. 'I can't believe there is time for every teacher to wade through it all so I'm asking everyone on the staff to take one area from this list and to become our reviewer, our editor and our reporter on that area.'

Each member of staff was asked to report each term to the rest on what was new, what was important and what decisions needed to be made. Becky, the newest arrival on the staff, took on technology as no-one else seemed keen on it. She found it quite hard work keeping up, particularly when the National Curriculum papers started to roll in. She also found rather daunting the knowledge that if she missed the importance of something, the whole school might suffer. Nevertheless, she did like it when even senior members of staff came to her for explanation of something they had seen in a newspaper. The day came when the staff were debating how to interrelate science and technology in the school curriculum plan. Becky and Jane, the science reader, put together a summary of the requirements of the two curriculum areas and a set of notes about the issues which arose as a consequence. At the staff meeting, the issues were decided one by one. Becky knew that without her work it would not have got anywhere.

Cameo 6.4: *Lyn and Barbara*

Lyn had been head of the school for three years, during the last two of which she had cautiously introduced an appraisal scheme. The staff were now making this work really well and morale and confidence had rocketed upwards.

Barbara had taken on the role of maths coordinator eighteen months ago and was just beginning to make things hum. Six months before her recent appraisal, Barbara had joined the LEA working group on assessment in mathematics on Lyn's recommendation because she knew the school had a lot to do in that area. At her appraisal they agreed that the production and implementation of a policy on assessment should be Barbara's major target for the following year.

A month later, Barbara asked Lyn whether the school could release her for one afternoon a week for a year in order to work with a small group of other teachers under the auspices of the LEA working group. They would produce guidelines and some working materials for all schools in the LEA.

Lyn hesitated. She didn't want to lose the impetus Barbara had created in the school. Nor did she want the LEA task to demand large quantities of Barbara's time and energy, as such jobs often do. On the other hand, it would be good for Barbara's career and there would be a lot of spin-off for the school. It would also be seen by others as a test of Lyn's commitment to appraisal targets. She agreed to bring in supply cover in order to allow Barbara to take part.

Cameo 6.5: *Fenland Primary School*

Fenland Primary School has a reputation as a fine school with a stable staff and a tradition of working as a team. It was one of the first schools in the County to have a school development plan. A cornerstone of that plan was that every teacher should become curriculum coordinator for one part of the curriculum.

The idea was that the staff as a whole would agree the broad curriculum then different areas would be developed by groups led by the curriculum coordinators. Each of these would be agreed by the whole staff group. Not only content would be agreed but also what we would now call attainment targets.

At the point where the curriculum was put into operation the agreed role of the coordinators changed. Each observed colleagues teaching their area of the curriculum, each gathered samples of pupils' work and each evaluated whether the objectives agreed by the whole staff for that area were being reached.

It worked well. The curriculum benefits were great, as the head had anticipated. What he hadn't expected was the increase in team teaching with people working in pairs across the whole staff. Attendance at INSET courses doubled in the year that followed. When a group of local heads came to hear about the scheme one evening, every member of staff turned out to support him.

Cameo 6.6:   *The area cluster*
Four tiny primary schools in a rural area far from anywhere decided that in order to provide their pupils with a wider experience they would develop their curricula together. They started with joint sporting and musical activities, then began to plan topic work across the four schools, using the greater expertise of the staff of all four. Soon it developed further and teachers from each of the schools began to do some teaching in the other three.

Teachers have managed to keep in balance the two loyalties — to school and cluster. They now have a dozen colleagues, instead of two, and they prefer it. The curriculum they offer is more satisfying. Morale is high — they feel they are moving forward.

---

to move them out of their present positions, but from the point of view of their career development it is a very good thing, as before deputy headship they will need to widen their portfolio of experience. For the school it may be no bad thing either. It shifts their enthusiasm and skills to a different area and it avoids the school's success in their original area from being associated only with their personal input.

Involvement in Evaluation

Evaluation demands the clear enunciation of objectives and the collection of data related to their achievement, followed by analysis and discussion. The freeing of ideas and the necessity to put these ideas to the test helps teachers to recognize that even if some prove unhelpful, they have actually moved forward in the process of trying them.

Involvement in Research and Development

Why is it that innovation projects always work in the trial schools, even if they break down when launched later upon other schools? Part of the answer is that in the trial schools the teachers were encouraged to evaluate each part of the proposed project and to suggest alterations which would improve it. As a result of this analysis, they were able to make it work better in their schools. They had developed as teachers through their involvement in the new project.

The same conclusion appears to be true of all innovatory work, whether developed outside the school or inside it. It is almost an argument for keeping a school in a state of continuing change for change's sake.

Used purposefully, all of these situations can be put to good use in staff development. The good manager is constantly looking for ways of building staff development into the regular life of the school. To help them extend that process managers have the support of many people outside the school, so that they can provide a regular programme of INSET courses, both in the school and outside it. That is the subject of the next chapter.

Chapter 7

Making Effective Use of Courses and Consultancies

The Goals of INSET

April 1st 1987 saw a permanent, irreversible change in the way IN-SET is run in this country, both in its organization and in its financing. The reasons for the impetus to change are very diverse and it may help us if we tease out the different goals sought by the variety of protagonists in the debate.

Teachers wanted	(i)	more funds for INSET;
	(ii)	more school-focused INSET;
	(iii)	more say in the sort of INSET provided.

LEAs wanted	(i)	INSET directly related to their goals;
	(ii)	to move the balance of INSET from serving the individual to serving the school;
	(iii)	more control over the activities provided, so that they could ensure the change;
	(iv)	to be freed from the inequalities of the pooling system, and from the reliance on long courses provided by higher education (HE) which that entailed.

What did the Government and Department of Education and Science want? When the new scheme was published, Circular 6/86 listed its main purposes:

    (i)   to promote the professional development of teachers;
    (ii)   to promote more systematic and purposeful planning of INSET;

(iii) to encourage more effective management of the teaching force;

(iv) to encourage training in selected national priority areas.

We can read between those lines the Government's wish to raise standards among teachers, to make the LEAs more accountable for their use of INSET funds and to direct INSET towards centrally-determined goals.

The challenge in the new system is to bring together these varied and sometimes conflicting agenda into an effective unity. We can demonstrate the growth of more systematic planning of INSET in LEAs and in schools, as we can demonstrate the encouragement of training in national priority areas. It is in the areas closest to the pupils — professional development of teachers and the development of schools — where we cannot as yet make claims with confidence.

In a DES report, Glickman and Dale (1990) quoted HMI findings (HMI, 1989) that

The introduction of the LEA Training Grants Scheme (LEATGS) has resulted in more systematic approaches to the planning, organization and delivery of INSET by the large majority of LEAs visited. In general terms INSET is now more healthy than it has been at any time previously, despite the various weaknesses identified in the first year of the new scheme. The LEA systems being put into place and gradually refined make them well placed to accommodate the challenge of providing the training necessary to help teachers and lecturers introduce the various changes required by the Education Reform Act.

However, they go on to say

There are weaknesses with LEATGS. It lends itself to cumbersome supervision. There is some concern that the management systems are not able to harness to best effect the particular expertise of higher education institutions. There is some disappointment, on the part of teachers and others, that LEATGS is not fulfilling its promise of promoting the professional development of teachers.

For anyone concerned with staff development this is a disappointing conclusion. Of the four Government objectives for INSET, the professional development of teachers must be the most important. The other three can only be fully successful if they contribute to the first. Improving the management structure may make INSET more efficient, but we can only claim it is more effective if it does bring about the development of teachers.

There is a critical decision to be made at this point and its outcome depends on how we believe change is accomplished. Some believe it can be directed, i.e. we decide the nature of the change and the teachers are seen as the means of delivering it, so our task is to decide the change and then train teachers to the necessary competence level. Others believe that real change only emerges when teachers have been active in developing it. Not for them the 'delivery man' model, they prefer to regard teachers like members of a design team. INSET then takes a very different shape because it is concerned with keeping ideas flowing and maintaining creativity. Change becomes a matter for management, not for direction.

It is likely that a few everyday items of change can be brought about using the 'delivery man' model, provided they do not conflict dramatically with the philosophy or teaching style of those concerned. If, however, the need for change challenges the teachers' beliefs or current practices then the 'design team' approach is likely to be necessary. It goes without saying that the coexistence of the two models gives rise to problems, particularly when teachers are asked to switch from one to another. The delivery men who are overnight transformed into a design team because their school is involved in a merger understandably have difficulties. So will the innovative primary school staff faced suddenly with a National Curriculum which asks them to act as delivery men.

For Whom and By Whom?

To help us explore different INSET possibilities, it is worth formulating aims for INSET that demonstrate how they serve the school and the teachers:

For the Individual

(i) To promote the professional development of the individual
   (a) maintenance function — be better at what they are doing now,
   (b) preparation function — be ready for what they will do in future.

For the School System

(ii) To equip schools to deliver what they set out to do now.
(iii) To help schools to develop their work for the future
    (a) in response to needs they identify,
    (b) in response to needs identified by the LEA,
    (c) in response to needs identified nationally.
(iv) To maintain and improve the supply of thinkers, developers and leaders for the future, including headteachers, advisers and administrators, researchers, evaluators and trainers.

We are then in a position to consider the most useful roles for INSET-providers inside and outside the school. The maintenance function for individuals and the school's present-day needs can be met economically, quickly and effectively by the schools and the LEAs provided that the skills and time for needs identification, designing an appropriate programme and providing the necessary support are available within the school and the LEA. Observing what has happened on some staff development days in schools, it is clear that while the potential and the aptitude are there in many schools, the skills of working with adults and the understanding of INSET design are often not. That knowledge is often available in the LEA but the time is not. Those skills are available in higher education (HE) institutions but not on a scale which would allow their use with individual schools on a one-to-one basis except in rare cases. It would be better use of HE to 'train the trainers', seeking to establish at least one person in each school with the appropriate level of skills, and preferably a team of them.

Developing the school's work for the future demands of teachers a series of skills:

(i) School needs identification — many schools now have these skills available, though many need extending.
(ii) Deciding priorities and managing the process of change. Still more management training is needed at senior level but there is a particular need at middle management level. Management training skills are thin in LEAs and schools, so this is a major field for externally-provided INSET.
(iii) Relating staff development to the process of change is also a management requirement.
(iv) Finally we come to the staff development processes. Desired outcomes may well include change of attitude or a

change of style, more difficult to achieve than change of content. This requires time and particular kinds of activity. HE has a major share of the skills and knowledge required and long courses continue to have a major part to play.

In the supply of future thinkers, developers and leaders, HE has played a major role in the past. There are not many alternatives and the need can hardly be challenged. This is, however, the area of INSET which has suffered most during the recent changes. It has suffered for two reasons. The first is that to develop the qualities required of future leaders demands time for reflection, exploration and development. It has usually been done through long award-bearing courses and these are expensive in time. The second reason is that activities of this kind do not, by their very nature, send course members back to school with a specific change to implement. Their benefits are more widely felt but their lack of immediate impact in the school often leads to the accusation that they are not useful. We need to develop some means of demonstrating the long-term impact of these longer courses.

INSET Design

Variety in Format

A single INSET activity can take many different forms. Its length can vary from a single lecture followed by discussion to a higher degree course lasting several years. It can be made up of a single continuous full-time block or can be composed of a series of events interspersed with normal work. It can take place in the school or outside it and it can be designed for the staff of a single school or take participants from many schools.

In deciding on the format for a particular INSET activity, the starting point has to be the aims which it is desired to achieve. These will also condition our expectations about the outcomes. Short activities may suffice to raise teachers' awareness of an issue but they may not be sufficient to influence their practice. The question of *what* to teach is a very much simpler INSET problem than *how* to teach but unfortunately most problems identified by schools involve the latter as well as the former.

The evidence from curriculum development projects in the 1970s suggests strongly that INSET has to match with the teacher's own goals, perceptions and style and to fit with the overall curriculum objectives of the school if it is to be successful. Yet in the 1980s we saw attempts at INSET on a national scale using the 'cascade process' in which some 'super trainers' passed the message to some ordinary trainers who passed it on to someone from each school who passed it on to the rest. Apart from the problems arising from the difficulty of transmitting a faithful message down the chain, the expectation that it matches teachers' goals and schools' situations was untested and often unjustified. Innovations could be observed to be faltering because their INSET was addressed to the surface issues while the stumbling blocks were at a much more fundamental level.

To be successful in meeting school goals, INSET must not only give a lead on what schools ought to do but also address the major question of how schools can get to the point where that is accepted and there is a desire to put it into practice. Such INSET is likely to be longer rather than shorter.

The desired goals also affect the other parameters of the format of INSET. There are very good reasons for approaching INSET as a whole staff when addressing some issues but there are other cases where involving individual teachers with others from outside the school is more beneficial. This may be because the variety of experience they bring is important or it may be because there are mistakes that might be made during training which are better made in a neutral but supportive atmosphere rather than under the gaze of colleagues.

It becomes important therefore not to develop a fixed adherence to one format for INSET, but to choose the format according to its purposes. It is equally important to give major attention to identification of participants' needs and to matching the INSET to them, not just in the broad sense of 'I want a course about science' but much more specifically than that. Part of this matching process extends to the briefing participants have from their school or LEA before joining the course and on the preparatory work which is required. One of the most striking pieces of evidence to arise from the management training opportunities stimulated in the 1980s by the Government was that the courses themselves were often greeted with enthusiasm but the briefing of members by their LEAs was often reported to be perfunctory so they arrived unprepared and not knowing why they were there.

Another aspect of INSET which is often neglected is that of follow-up afterwards. There is always the need to follow the course through into action and implementation, with further support should that prove necessary. All too often the outcomes of the course, even school-based and school-focused courses, are lost as the teachers plunge back into the hurly-burly of school life.

In a report for the National Foundation for Educational Research, Bolam (1987) summarized the findings of a number of research and development studies and suggested that good courses of INSET have the following features:

* collaborative planning involving course leaders, LEA sponsors and former or prospective participants;
* a clear focus upon participants' current and future needs;
* careful preparatory briefing for participants several weeks ahead of the course, with opportunities for pre-course work where appropriate;
* a programme which is structured but has enough flexibility to allow for modifications in the light of monitoring and formative evaluation;
* a programme which is oriented towards experience, practice and action, and using, as appropriate, methods like action learning, action research, performance feedback and on-the-job assistance;
* a 'sandwich' timetable including course-based and job-based experiences to facilitate this approach;
* careful de-briefing after the course and sustained support, ideally including on-the-job assistance where new skills are being implemented.

Variety in Content

Just as it is important to choose the format of an INSET activity according to the purpose intended, so we need to consider in the same way the construction of the elements which make up the activity. If the maxim 'the medium is the message' is not always the complete story, then it is certainly true that the medium must support and reinforce the message.

An INSET course about participatory decision-making which is conducted through a series of lectures carries its own contradictory message. An INSET activity is therefore likely to be made up of a variety of elements, with different purposes:

* presenting information,
* establishing data,

* raising awareness,
* enhancing skills,
* discussing alternative possibilities,
* changing attitudes.

It follows that within one INSET activity, teachers will experience a variety of different styles of working, involving exercises as well as listening and discussing. Very often exercises are used to open up an area or issue, as they are in children's learning. Skilful INSET providers often use a lot of elements within an activity, assuming that their clients' attention span will be short, not because they are stupid but because they are creative and want to explore the new idea with colleagues before proceeding to the next. Thus new ideas are interspersed with opportunities to explore them.

In creating a programme, there are three things to remember:

Seek	* variety of activities,
	* balance of activities,
	* progress towards goals which are clear to the participants,
	* understanding among participants of the purpose of each activity.
Remember	* attention spans are limited,
	* breaks can be a disturbance, or they can be used positively.
Provide	* guidance material for participants,
	* back-up instructions for group leaders,
	* suggestions for getting started.

The attitudes and expectations which participants bring with them to the INSET activity often facilitate or limit what can be achieved. Sometimes these attitudes and expectations are external to the participants. They are created by the Government, the LEA or the community and they can be sufficient to overwhelm all other considerations. Thus worry over local financial management or a school closure can prevent teachers from giving their minds to a curriculum issue which at other times they would regard as very important.

An alternative influence on attitudes and expectations exists within the participants and arises from the question 'Why do I want to go?'. Maybe the ideal INSET participant answers 'Because there are bits of my performance I want to improve' but it would be foolish to assume that would be the universal response. Others attend out of loyalty to their staff or because they have been sent by LEA or school, sometimes with enthusiasm, sometimes not. Another group, the 'country club', attend for social purposes or out of habit — 'the heads *always* go to Clacton for two days', 'staff development days are the only times we have to talk to one another'. A third group attends activities in order to achieve qualifications or pass some hurdle on the route to promotion.

These groups are likely to react differently to the activities they are offered, some giving more effort and accepting a higher level of commitment than others. Participants sometimes shy away from participatory exercises in which their own performance comes under scrutiny. They may prefer the lecture format from which they can safely distance themselves with the comment that 'it doesn't apply to our school'.

It is, of course, possible to explore these predispositions in the preparatory work leading up to the INSET activity, either through correspondence with the participant and his or her school:

> 'Please write me a short letter explaining your hopes and expectations of the course and issues which currently exercise you',

or in negotiation with the planning group for the activity. Experience shows it is very important to write down the expectations which trainer, trainee and funder have of each other in a kind of three-way contract.

The 'write me a letter' approach to participants has threefold usefulness — it helps the planning of appropriate activities, it can be used in the briefing of group leaders as an introduction to their group members and it can be a useful reminder of their starting point when individuals are asked to evaluate the activity.

There are two major purposes which are addressed by most INSET activities, sometimes separately, sometimes together. They are

> * awareness-raising or eye opening,
>   and
> * enhancing skills and understanding.

Sadly, quite a lot of INSET activities achieve only the first of these when the organizers hoped they were addressing the second. Hopefully, the reasons why this is so will become apparent in the discussion which follows.

Awareness-raising

INSET activities which are geared towards awareness-raising help teachers to become aware of

* some new development,
* some concern which other people have,
* some deficiency in their performance or that of their school.

In doing so there is likely to be some conflict with the teachers' present perceptions.

At the end of an awareness-raising activity, the participants may be able to do something about the focus of concern if they already have the skills and resources to do so. The activity itself, however, has not given them the skills and understanding required and, where they do not already exist, further INSET will be necessary.

A number of possible exercises can be used to raise awareness:

Practice exercises without repetition. It is not unusual to draw attention to the importance of a particular skill in an awareness-raising course by asking participants to take part in an exercise which demands its use. Example 7.1, an exercise on listening and summarizing, is a typical example.

As it stands, the exercise makes the assumptions that, having done the exercise, A and B will recognize any deficiencies there might be in their own performances and that they will be able to go away and put them right. The exercise would be developed further by introducing training in those particular skills and repetition of similar exercises to consolidate them. It would then become an exercise in skills enhancement.

Example 7.1   *Listening and summarizing*

Participants will work in pairs, A and B.

* A should talk for two minutes about the kind of holidays he or she likes.
* B should concentrate on listening and on using non-verbal means of showing interest and encouraging A.
* B should then summarize in one minute the points A has made, in doing so ensuring that A's meaning has been fully grasped.
* The roles should now be reversed, with B talking about why he or she chose teaching as a career, and A doing the listening and summarizing.
* A and B should then spend 10–15 minutes agreeing and listing the important factors which contribute to:

(i)   good listening skills,
(ii) good summarizing.

Pupil pursuit. In this kind of exercise, a teacher shadows a pupil or a group of pupils for an extended period making notes of what they do and what happens to them. The brief can be open or structured according to the teacher's concerns. Example 7.2 is an interesting example of one structured approach.

Observing and being observed. Much has already been said about the value of observation in earlier chapters. It is sufficient to remark here that observation, like many exercises, contributes only to awareness-raising unless it is followed by further skill-development activities.

Example 7.2

The Received Curriculum — The Pupil's Eye View

We can spend many an hour putting together teaching schemes, preparing lessons and collecting together resources. Ultimately what counts most is the value of all these experiences from the pupil's point of view. Do they learn any better with arrangement A than with arrangement B? What is their day like? Do they sit through hours of teacher-talk? Do they spend all day staring at workcards? Are they always in the same group, large or small? Are they passive or active? Do they talk, and to whom? Do they read or write much in a day? Do they concentrate on the task in hand or is their time wasted? Are they experiencing a balance of subjects?

These and a thousand other questions can be asked about the curriculum as the pupils experience it. Our experience with hundreds of headteachers and senior staff in schools in England is that all too seldom do they find time to observe over a length of time the experience they have planned for pupils being put into practice. Their responses to doing the task — 'very revealing', 'conscience-tugging', 'I learned the difference between what I thought was happening and the reality' — indicate their surprise at its outcomes.

For this task we ask you to observe a class of pupils for as long a period as you feel will give you an adequate picture of their received curriculum. During this time we ask you to undertake three tasks:

(i)   a work involvement study of *all* pupils,
(ii) individual studies of *two* pupils,
(iii) a curriculum content study

Work Involvement Study

During the lessons you observe choose two occasions when children are supposed to be busy at some task. In each case ask yourself two questions:

(i) is the pupil involved in the task?
(ii) is he/she misbehaving?

Move steadily around the class taking pupils at a time and watching them closely for *TWENTY SECONDS*. At the end of this time tick the observation sheet for that pupil.

Suppose pupil 1 is highly involved in the task and is not misbehaving, pupil 2 spends little time at work and chatters (mild misbehaviour), pupil 3 shows medium involvement but punches the person next to him during the twenty seconds (more serious misbehaviour) you would tally the observation sheet as follows:

Pupil	Seconds on task (out of 20)			Level of Misbehaviour		
	Low 0–5	Medium 6–15	High 16–20	More Serious	Mild	None
1			✔			✔
2	✔				✔	
3		✔		✔		
4						
5						

The level of involvement is decided by the number of seconds the pupils appear to be applying themselves to the task in hand. Thus 0–5 seconds denotes low, 6–15 seconds medium, and 16–20 seconds high involvement.

Remember this only gives a *rough and ready* indication of pupils' involvement and is not an accurate means of comparing one teacher with another. This is not the purpose of this activity. The central purpose is to allow you to scrutinize the class on two occasions and see what each pupil is doing. You will see far more than is represented by the tallies in the observation sheet.

Individual Pupil Study

For this exercise you need to choose *two* pupils, preferably one you know to be hard-working and interested in lessons and another who is the reverse. At some time during each lesson or period of thirty or forty minutes watch only these two pupils for *five minutes* each. Make freehand notes on the sheet provided describing what each pupil does.

	PUPIL A	PUPIL B
LESSON 1	Reads work cards (1/2 minute). Writes answer. Fetches dictionary. Looks up definition. Asks teacher what to do next. Makes start on homework (reading about the Rockies) (2 minutes).	Waiting in line to see teacher (1 minute). Has work marked. Returns to seat. Chatters with neighbour. Moves over to adjacent group and interrupts their work. Scolded by teacher. Ignores reprimand and continues to distract others.

Curriculum Content Study

Recent HMI documents have defined eight areas of the curriculum. We consider here their relative emphases for the class you observe. At the end of each lesson fill in the grid below, showing where the balance of activities lay. For example, if a great deal of time was spent on social matters, either for the whole group or in small groups, assign a score of 3 to that area, and so on.

	Lesson 1	Lesson 2	Lesson 3	Lesson 4	TOTAL
1. Aesthetic/ creative					
2. Ethical					
3. Linguistic					
4. Mathematical					
5. Physical					
6. Scientific					
7. Social/ political					
8. Spiritual					

Key Insert 0, 1, 2, 3 in each cell.
   3 = The major area covered in the lesson.
   2 = An area which received some significant degree of attention.
   1 = An area which received a little attention.
   0 = An area which received no attention.

e.g. One might watch a maths lesson, and then score it as follows.

	Lesson 1
Aesthetic/creative	1
Ethical	0
Linguistic	0
Mathematical	3
Physical	0
Scientific	1
Social/political	0
Spiritual	0

At the end of the day

Look at the grand totals for each one. There is, of course, no reason why they should all be equal. Indeed you may not have been able to see a balanced programme in the time you have available. Nevertheless look at the balance *of what you have seen*, and reflect on its appropriateness for the group concerned.

Collecting and analyzing data. Any form of data collection and analysis has the potential for identifying new issues and in the context of INSET it is a very useful way of developing participants' ownership of the issues. Participants react much more warmly to activities which are seen to address problems they have identified than to activities which tell them they have those problems.

Role-play and simulation. There are always some members of any group who find role-play threatening or who feel it makes demands on acting skills they may not have. Nevertheless, many teachers who experience it find it a very powerful experience in raising their awareness. An atmosphere of trust, both in the INSET leader and fellow participants, is obviously helpful in bringing success. Choosing the subject for role play to be close to the experience of participants, so that they can act as they would normally and not act an alien role, also helps.

Games. There is a wide variety of games available which alert participants to the issues involved in planning, in collaborating, in decision-making and other managerial activities. The exercise illustrated in Example 7.3 is a typical example. Other games illustrate other issues, for example what it is like to be perpetually underprivileged or to be isolated.

There are some real exercises which achieve the same aims as games. Many of them involve the construction of something against a performance brief. They are much used in management training and often have a competitive element.

Enhancing Skills and Understanding

One set of activities which enhances skills involves situations in which groups 'brainstorm' possible solutions and then analyze their likely effectiveness, putting individuals in the position where they have the chance to test their ideas against the scrutiny of others. Another set consists of different kinds of observation and feedback exercises.

Examples 7.4 and 7.5 are typical short exercises of the first kind. The first helps people to recognize the different kinds of question and then sets out to develop their skills in choosing those that are more useful. The second example enhances skills in solving problems. The presenters of the problems have the advantage of hearing new minds address their problem, the others have the challenge of having to react quickly to a new problem.

Discussion of cameos and case studies which present a problem to be solved are also useful in this work, as are accounts of 'critical incidents' like that in Example 7.6 which is one of a series devised to help trainee teachers consider their relationships with other teachers.

The second group of activities has observation and feedback as its central feature. Careful briefing of the observer is necessary. Example 7.7 illustrates a typical role-play exercise with a rather loose briefing for the observer. Example 7.8 presents a more detailed

Example 7.3

Winter Survival Exercise: The Situation

You have just crash-landed in the woods of northern Minnesota and southern Manitoba. It is 11:32 A.M. in mid-January. The light plane in which you were traveling crashed on a lake. The pilot and copilot were killed. Shortly after the crash the plane sank completely into the lake with the pilot's and copilot's bodies inside. None of you are seriously injured and you are all dry.

The crash came suddenly, before the pilot had time to radio for help or inform anyone of your position. Since your pilot was trying to avoid a storm, you know the plane was considerably off course. The pilot announced shortly before the crash that you were twenty miles northwest of a small town that is the nearest known habitation.

You are in a wilderness area made up of thick woods broken by many lakes and streams. The snow depth varies from above the ankles in windswept areas to knee-deep where it has drifted. The last weather report indicated that the temperature would reach minus twenty-five degrees Fahrenheit in the daytime and minus forty at night. There is plenty of dead wood and twigs in the immediate area. You are dressed in winter clothing appropriate for city wear — suits, pantsuits, street shoes, and overcoats.

While escaping from the plane the several members of your group salvaged twelve items. Your task is to rank these items according to their importance to your survival, starting with *1* for the most important item and ending with *12* for the least important one.

You may assume that the number of passengers is the same as the number of persons in your group, and that the group has agreed to stick together.

Rank the following items according to their importance to your survival, starting with *1* for the most important one and proceeding to *12* for the least important one.

— Ball of steel wool
— Newspapers (one per person)
— Compass
— Hand ax
— Cigarette lighter (without fluid)
— Loaded .45-caliber pistol
— Sectional air map made of plastic
— Twenty-by-twenty-foot piece of heavy-duty canvas
— Extra shirt and pants for each survivor
— Can of shortening
— Quart of 100-proof whiskey
— Family-size chocolate bar (one per person)

Procedure

Group members are asked to construct their individual list of importance from 1 to 12. Then they are invited to debate the priorities as a group and to reach consensus on a group ranking of the 12 items.

After constructing these two lists they are provided with an 'ideal solution' and by calculating the total differences between individual rankings and ideal rankings, group and ideal rankings and individual and group rankings they can explore:

(i) whether they got nearer to the best solution by working as a group;
(ii) why it was that some individuals had better solutions than that finally adopted by the group. Why were they not heeded by the group?
(iii) what were productive and unproductive strategies for reaching good solutions and whether they were the same as strategies for reaching consensus.

Source: David W. Johnson and Frank P. Johnson, *Joining Together: Group Theory and Group Skills*, 2nd edition, (c) 1982, p. 355. Reprinted by permission of Prentice Hall, Englewood Cliffs, New Jersey.

Example 7.4

Questioning

* Each individual in the group should spend 10 minutes creating questions in each of the categories identified by Hewton (1988) and listed below.
* In groups of four or five, examine the examples in each category. What is it that typifies questions in that category?
* What can you do to increase the number of open and reflective questions you ask?

Question Types

Closed	— establishes facts, discourages elaboration. 'Did you take it?'
Open	— encourages the person to explore the issue in whatever way they wish. 'What did you think was going on?' 'What should we do?'
Reflective	— invites the person to think about his or her feelings or beliefs. 'You said you were pleased with the answer.' 'How did you feel about winning?'
Probing	— seeks to extend a previous answer. 'Is it significant that it was Friday?' 'What else affects it?'
Leading	— seeks agreement with the questioner. 'I'm sure you were tired, is that right?'
Multiple	— asks several things at once. 'Do you dislike sex and violence?'

Example 7.5

How Would You Handle This One?

Participants work in groups of four or five.

A describes a situation which presents him or her with a professional problem, taking three to four minutes.

The rest of the group (the Bs) then discuss how they would resolve the situation. A is not allowed to contribute to this discussion except to supply facts on request. They have ten minutes to reach a conclusion.

The task is then repeated with another person in the A role until all have presented a problem.

briefing sheet prepared for a group of observers who were about to watch a group of colleagues engaged in a simulated staff meeting. Example 7.9 is a briefing sheet for three teachers involved in training for the appraisal interview. The briefing spells out the roles each should take. The next example, 7.10, shows a typical briefing for visits conducted by course members in pairs to each other's schools. Finally Example 7.11 is an example of the observer's brief for analyzing the quality of feedback in telerecorded classroom observation and feedback sessions.

Features of Effective INSET

In this last section on the design of INSET, it is worth reminding ourselves of the work of Joyce and Showers (1980) in the United States. They suggest a hierarchy of aspects of INSET:

* presentation of theory, description of skill;
* demonstration or modelling;
* practice, simulated or real;
* feedback about performance;
* coaching, in the classroom, with emphasis on repetition for improvement,

Example 7.6

An Example of a Critical Incident

Timothy Dumont — Junior School Teacher in his Probationary Year

I feel now that I have established what I call 'my discipline' — it is not a disorderly class. You can come in, you can find it noisy but at the same time if I just say 'stop' they all stop and go back to their places, they'll sit down and they'll shut up more or less. I can have it noisy when I wish, then we can get down to some quiet, possibly boring work and they take it all in their stride. But I have run into trouble over this class with another member of the staff who has been teaching thirty years. On Wednesdays we have the use of the local swimming pool. It is a nice heated one and I go in swimming with them and put them through their paces with their various swimming certificates. I go in with them and some of them have said to this teacher 'Oh, we ducked Sir this morning'. It was all done in very good fun. She said to me, 'I don't see how you can have any respect among those children when you allow them to do that to you'. I snapped back at her, 'I've got more respect from them now than you'll ever have!' Well, I was nettled so I fired from the hip, you might say. But this is the attitude. There are certain things which are taboo — you must not allow the children to duck you in the swimming pool, in fact you mustn't go in with them at all.

Based on an account in Hannam, C., Smyth, P. and Stephenson, N. (1976) *The First Year of Teaching*, Harmondsworth, Penguin.

Example 7.7

Separate briefs for the two active participants and the observer in a short role-play.

Briefing for Headteacher

You have been asked to talk with B who has been applying for deputy headships which in all honesty you cannot support although you have never said this openly. B began a teaching career at the school eight years ago, and was asked by your predecessor to take responsibility for audiovisual aids and Games. The level of commitment by B to the school is acceptable with courses attended especially on physical education and Games. B's overall classroom organization and teaching is sound without being exciting — the relationships with the rest of the staff show an abrasive side to B's personality, yet there is potential for development if B would listen to advice, mature a little and show greater application. You want to use this interview as an opportunity to explain that B's classroom teaching could be more creative and exciting, while suggesting that a sideways move may be more appropriate than a deputy headship at this stage.

Briefing for Teacher

You have been invited by the head to discuss your career prospects after a number of unsuccessful applications for deputy headship. So far you have had no interviews. You began your teaching career at this school eight years ago, have responsibility for audiovisual aids and Games (but no allowance) and work hard. You would be happy to draw up some school guidelines for physical education and wonder if anyone would ever use them! At present you feel a bit fed-up with teaching and are wondering whether to try something else (especially as you are single with no family ties).

Observer's Observation Proforma

Using the form, note the ways in which the Headteacher demonstrates his/her concern or lack of concern, ability or lack of ability to help the teacher. Please note both non-verbal and verbal signals.

Helping signals from Headteacher	Non-helping signals from Headteacher and/or Teacher	Practical help/guidance offered by Headteacher
1.	1.	1.
2.	2.	2.
3.	3.	3.
4.	4.	4.
5.	5.	5.
6.	6.	6.
7.	7.	7.
8.	8.	8.
9.	9.	9.
10.	10.	10.
11.	11.	11.
12.	12.	12.
13.	13.	13.
14.	14.	14.
15.	15.	15.

Example 7.8

Observation of Group Discussion

Note: It is necessary to develop methods of recording your observations appropriate to what is being observed.

1. Observers will be given specific tasks from among the following:
   (a) Spoken exchanges between members (e.g. frequency; who speaks to whom)
   (b) Non-verbal interaction, e.g. facial expression, body gestures, orientation and voice intonation
   (c) Non-verbal devices for signalling and attracting attention when waiting to speak, e.g. coughing, leaning forward, hand-raising
   (d) Occurrence of certain patterns of behaviour, e.g.:
       (i) 'Chairperson' behaviour by members of the group (e.g. drawing together or summing up group thinking, teaching, clarifying)
       (ii) Supportive/non-supportive behaviour by members of the group towards others
       (iii) Isolation of members by others and the resolution of this
       (iv) The group's treatment of the leader
       (v) The timing of sections of the discussion
2. The verbal and non-verbal behaviour of the leader:
   (a) How does the leader deal with the structure of the discussion? In particular:
       (i) Introduction
       (ii) Getting started
       (iii) Summing up and moving on
       (iv) Conclusions
   (b) How does the leader deal with interaction problems? e.g.:
       (i) The over-talkative and the over-silent member
       (ii) Pairing which goes on too long
       (iii) Aggression, conflict, other emotionally tense situations
       (iv) The member who becomes isolated
   (c) What sort of relationship does the leader establish with each group member?
   (d) What are the leader's strengths? What does the leader need to work at?

Example 7.9

Triads

In this exercise, appraiser and appraisee will be observed discussing an area of performance identified by the appraisee. The exercise is done in threes (triads) and each in turn acts as appraiser, appraisee and observer. In preparation each shares about a page of writing with the other two, concerning the selected area of performance. The benefits of the exercise are for

(i) the appraiser, who has the chance to practice handling a discussion of this kind in safe and controlled circumstances,
and
(ii) the observer, who has the chance to analyze the performance of the appraiser and also the chance to practice feedback afterwards.

The appraiser

* chairs
* listens
* encourages
* summarizes
* leads

The appraisee

* explains
* explores
* focuses
* considers possible actions

The observer

* watches the appraiser in action
* records
* feeds back observations

Example 7.10

Paired Visits to Schools

Purpose of visits: to examine communications between adults in the host school and to write a brief report on these for the host headteacher.

Suggested Activities

Each member should choose, after consultation with his/her host, *three* or *four* of these activities.

1. Examine the staff room noticeboard and other relevant sources of written communication.
2. Observe verbal and non-verbal interaction between head and teachers; between teachers; and between both these groups and the non-teaching staff.
3. Observe occasions (e.g. assembly, staff meetings) when the head communicates formally with the teachers.
4. Interview two or three parents or parent helpers to discover their views on e.g.:
   — the school brochure and its effectiveness.
   — the newsletters and circulars sent out to them.
   — parent evenings and meetings.
   — parent associations.
   — the effectiveness of communication as a parent-helper.
5. Interview two or three teachers and at least one member of the non-teaching staff to discover their views on, e.g.:
   — by what means does the head communicate with teaching and non-teaching staff?
   — what is his/her preferred mode of communication?
   — how effectively does he/she (a) transmit (b) receive information?
   — does the head remember what he/she has been told? Is there a good 'information-retrieval' system in the school?
   — does the head distinguish effectively between 'public' and 'private' information?
   — if members of the teaching/non-teaching staff want to communicate with the head, when and where do they find it most effective to do so?
   — when and where do teachers most often communicate with one another/with members of the non-teaching staff?
   — is such communication effective?
   — who seems to know most about what is going on in the school? How does he/she find out?
   — what should be done to improve communications within the school?
   — anything else that seems relevant and/or important.
6. Interview the headteacher, asking broadly the same questions, to provide a basis for comparison between the views of the teaching staff, the non-teaching staff and the head.
7. Arrange beforehand with your host to observe and/or examine in detail any particular aspect of communication within the school about which he/she wants further information.

Jobs for the Host

1. Explain to colleagues what is going to happen, and what they are being asked to do.
2. Prepare any necessary information for the visitor and supply him/her with it in advance.
3. For suggested activities 4 and 5, choose the teaching, non-teaching staff and parents for interviews, and make the necessary arrangements.
4. Identify the area to be examined in suggested activity 7, and discuss with the visitor the methods to be adopted. Make the necessary arrangements.

Jobs for the Visitor

1. Read any information provided by the host.
2. Decide how you will tackle suggested activities 4, 5 and 6.
3. Contact the host to discuss arrangements and to reach agreement on what is to be done, particularly for suggested activity 7.
4. Carry out detailed planning for suggested activities 1–7.
5. Carry out the visit.
6. Prepare a short written report for the host on communication between adults in the school, and let him/her have it well in advance of the next group meeting.

Example 7.11

Observing feedback

1. How does the observer try to establish a climate which will encourage discussion and the teacher's development?
2. How much did each talk? Was the balance of contribution helpful in reaching conclusions?
3. How far was the observer able to use data from the observation during the discussion? Did he/she usually use actual observed facts, or inferences and judgments?
4. How were nettles grasped? How was praise given and was it supported by reasons? In either case was there any half-heartedness?
5. Did he/she help the teacher to explore alternative possibilities?
6. How did they handle discussion about feelings?
7. What strategies did the observer use to maintain the pace of the discussion?
8. How did the observer help the teacher establish points for action? Who produced the proposals for action? Was it clear who was going to take the various actions?

and their results suggest that practical implementation of the theory or skill in the classroom depends upon use of the whole of this list. Without coaching, the effectiveness of INSET in their experiments was much impaired.

The implication of Joyce and Showers' work is major for it is coaching which takes time and is therefore expensive. It suggests that INSET will be longer rather than shorter if it is to affect classroom practice. It may be that we need to explore much more systematically the possibility of devising courses which have school-based or distance learning elements, so that tuition and on-the-job coaching can be combined more effectively.

INSET Which Links Personal Development and School Development

Accepting the earlier description that adults learn when their current observations are to some degree dissonant with their established concepts, the type of INSET most likely to make the link between personal and school development is one which asks the teachers to use the problem of developing their schools' practice as the vehicle for their own learning. There are now many examples of courses which combine elements of traditional learning with elements of action research. They come in many guises. There are Master's Degree and Advanced Diploma courses in applied research which not only introduce teachers to the study of the process but also incorporate a substantial action research component. There are also many examples of shorter courses, some school-based, some partly in school, partly outside, which gather data in schools before an aspect of study is begun. Others are involved in a development throughout the process, providing help and support at critical times during the development.

There is growing evidence that activities of this kind which are very much based on observational data invoke a different response from participants towards the need to change practice. A typical example emerged during Bradley and Eggleston's (1975) work concerning teachers during their induction year. When they first drew the attention of LEAs and headteachers to the national survey data published by Taylor and Dale (1971) the response was a remarkable consensus that although there was undoubtedly a problem nationally, in the LEAs and schools concerned there were adequate and successful systems of care for the new teacher. However, when groups of headteachers and LEA advisers were brought together in a course with an action research element, armed with some interview techniques and sent out to talk to probationary teachers in their own schools and others over a lengthy period, their change of view was substantial. They returned to the course clearly persuaded that there were problems and able to identify the young teachers' perceptions of them. There was now a will to address the problems. As a result, schools changed their support systems and each LEA substantially reorganized its system of welcoming, visiting and training new teachers.

Important factors in the success of this approach were the drawing of the schools and LEAs into partnership so that they felt the investigation was really theirs, and the encouragement to participants to go and find out for themselves. Once participants had established that there were problems, the INSET part of the activity could be addressed to those problems and could be made immediately relevant to them.

Although this activity was successful in bringing about change in the practice of schools and LEAs, there is a cautionary anecdote which illustrates one of INSET's perennial problems. Six of the primary heads in this experiment belonged to a cluster of twelve schools and carried out their investigations in all twelve. At the end of the work, the six who had been involved fed back their findings to the other six. To their surprise, they found their findings rejected. Their colleagues said, 'Yes, there is a national problem, but not in our schools ...' This is the INSET problem. Can we only learn through involvement? Is there no alternative to everyone individually re-inventing the wheel?

The example above concerns a short course. School-oriented long courses also raise issues for those who run them and those who take part in them. It is not enough simply to build a school development or research element into the course, even if teacher commitment to it is gained. If, as a result of the work, teachers recognize what needs to be done but are not empowered to do it, professional frustration follows. The nature of the exercise has to be the subject of a three-cornered negotiation between teacher, INSET provider and school. Carrying out this negotiation is not easy. Should you expect a commitment from the school to implement an as-yet unknown change? How many people might be involved in this commitment? Is it possible to find an issue which the school needs clarifying and which the teacher can handle in the time scale of the course?

A longer-term problem is finding answers to whether there have been permanent changes in practice, by individuals or by schools. Some course members arrive needing no conversion; they gain from the course the knowledge and skills they needed, contact with like minds, support for their experimentation and a stimulus to extend their thinking. For them, the course provides reinforcement and accelerates their progress. Other teachers arrive with a limited frame of reference and find the course allows them to make a quantum jump in their thinking and practice. Some are energized by the course into achieving something out of the ordinary and retain that level in further work, others return to their accustomed practice after the initial experience. Some, sadly, remain roughly where they were. Even among them, there is often evidence of a greater tolerance of the innovatory efforts of others so there is at least a limited gain.

Permanence of the change in the school appears to be most likely if:

* the individual is in a senior position;
* the research is sponsored by the staff and they identify with it;
* the research design treats other members of staff as re-searchers, not as data;
* there is support from the school management;
* the school has a tradition of investigatory work;
* there is active encouragement from the LEA.

Consultancy and the Role of the Consultant

Placing the responsibility for their development more in the hands of schools has enabled a school to identify a need for a course provided solely for its staff, or a functioning group within its staff. If schools wish to use expertise from outside their own staff, several possibilities are open to them:

(i) to 'buy' from a provider an 'off-the-shelf' course to be arranged on the school premises or nearby for staff from that school;

(ii) to 'buy' from the LEA or an HE institution the time of a consultant to plan and provide a course designed specifically for the school;

(iii) to send one or more members of the school staff on an attachment to an institution with the brief to develop a course for the school and the skills to provide it. This arrangement could include a limited amount of consultancy work within the school by staff of the institution.

In addition to this support at a distance there is a need in many cases for active support by a consultant in the school itself or in a group of schools, working alongside staff on their development issues or help-ing them to evaluate.

What can the outsider offer? The Support for Innovation Project (1989) considered this in its Issue Paper 3 'Helping Schools Help Themselves'. The Project suggests the following ways in which consultants or other external agents can offer support.

* Process consultancy
  How to set about the process of staff development or curri-culum development, where to begin and how to manage it.

* Critical friendship
  Offering an objective view, someone to bounce ideas off. Offering the chance to share the strains and the triumphs of innovation with an outsider who has a commitment to the school.
* Validation
  Bringing knowledge that other schools share the problem. Giving encouragement and praise. Reflecting progress made.
* Internal and external linkage
  Bringing the school into networks of good practice.
* Expert advice
  Because they know the school situation well, consultants are likely to be able to give very precise advice.
* Hands-on support
  Because of the continuing relationship with the school, the consultant can take part in the full Joyce and Showers (1980) hierarchy of INSET stages, including the all-important coaching.

The Project points out that external agents walk a fine line when helping schools in their development between offering support for the school's ideas and pressing their own ideas, even to the extent of creating dependency. The Project team described the tensions they felt in the consultancy role. Their summary of the tensions is a very useful way to end this chapter as it defines the advantages of the use of a consultant but also the pitfalls:

Advantages of being non-interventionist:
1   The need for schools to develop their own planning and organization of staff development so that it remains theirs, and continues when you go away.
2   To ensure that it is part of an on-going programme which is not dependent on an outsider; to ensure schools develop their own management structures, at all levels, for enabling and nurturing staff development.
3   Schools are in a better position than outsiders to develop means of addressing needs of members of staff who are suspicious of, and resistant to, outsiders interfering in the school. This resistance may manifest itself as diversionary tactics or direct opposition. It is sometimes better to withdraw in such cases.

4   Staff feel it is a great help to have an outsider to bounce their own ideas off, to be a 'sounding board' to help them focus their own ideas, and that this is a concrete enough action.

5   The experience gained during a process of staff development activities will probably help staff create a working framework suitable for them and their institution given time. Each person and each institution has different characteristics and the time taken depends on these individual factors.

6   Every member of staff has something to offer her/his colleagues and this can be encouraged, rather than handing over to an outside 'expert'.

7   Recognizing the possible limitations of support in the future thus not raising expectations which cannot be met.

Temptations to intervene:

1   To try to ensure that the school's planning and organization of INSET becomes an important and integral aspect of its development.

2   The need to empower, i.e. involve all members of staff, to allow them responsibility and freedom of choice, to ensure grass roots participation.

3   When there is resistance by some schools/staff whether this be in the form of direct opposition, or by diversionary tactics.

4   On a personal level, to feel that you are actually 'doing' something useful.

5   Personal professional accountability — it is difficult to sit back and watch specific events/activities go less well than they might had there been intervention.

6   The need to be seen to be doing something in order to justify to the school that their time and energy are being repaid in some concrete way.

7   The wish to work with individual teachers.

8   The wish to speed things up.

References

BOLAM, R. (1987) *What is Effective INSET?* Mimeo.

BRADLEY, H.W. and EGGLESTON, J.F. (1975) *An Enquiry into the Induction Year*, Nottingham, University of Nottingham School of Education.

DEPARTMENT OF EDUCATION AND SCIENCE (1986) *Circular 6/86: LEA Training Grants Scheme 1987–88*, London, HMSO.

GLICKMAN, B.D. and DALE, H.C. (1990) *A Scrutiny of Education Support Grants and the Local Education Authority Training Grants Scheme*, London, HMSO.

HER MAJESTY'S INSPECTORATE (1989) *The Implementation of the LEA Training Grant Scheme: report on the first year of the scheme 1987–88*, London, HMSO.

HEWTON, E. (1988) *The Appraisal Interview*, Milton Keynes, Open University Press.

JOYCE, B. and SHOWERS, B. (1980) 'Improving in-service training: the messages of research', *Educational Leadership*, February 1980, pp. 379–385.

SUPPORT FOR INNOVATION PROJECT (1989) *Thinking Schools*, Cambridge, Cambridge Institute of Education.

TAYLOR, J.K. and DALE, R. (1971) *A Survey of Teachers in their First Year of Service*, Bristol, University of Bristol School of Education.

Chapter 8

Managing the Process of Staff Development

Managers and Their Roles

The school must take the main responsibility for developing its capacity to manage. Developing the quality, motivation and organization of the school's human resources must stand alongside policy development and the evaluation of school performance as one of the principal areas of personal account-ability for the head, and a major concern for governors in monitoring and guiding progress. (DES, (1990) *Developing School Management — The Way Forward*)

There is little dissent from the view that staff development is one of the key areas in which headteachers and other senior staff should operate. The statement above from the School Management Task Force reminds us that managers need to take responsibility for three aspects of that work:

* motivating staff towards staff development;
* enhancing the quality of staff development activities and the receptiveness of the organization towards their outcomes;
* ensuring that staff development is an adequate resource for school development.

It was suggested in an earlier chapter that teachers risk the uncertainties and insecurities inherent in attempts at innovation because

(i) being involved in such activities, solving problems and overcoming challenges gives them continuing and rewarding job satisfaction, and

(ii)   engaging in these activities enhances their prospects of career development.

These two driving forces are very important for managers to consider when they address the three aspects of their staff development responsibility identified above. A series of questions for headteachers and other senior managers emerges from this consideration:

* How can we ensure that each teacher is offered a sufficient but not overwhelming supply of opportunities and challenges?
* How can the organization of the school be used, and if necessary changed, so as to maximize the effectiveness of staff development? How can blockages be removed, or better still anticipated and avoided? How can staff development be monitored?
* How can we use the evaluation and development of school performance in support of staff development as well as using staff development to support school development? How can we establish a shared understanding about what needs to be achieved and then manage staff in ways which increase the chance of its achievement?

The School Management Task Force Report, discussing the characteristics of successful school management, puts forward the following attributes:

(i)   a commitment to improving the learning of all students; clear purposes, goals and values shared by all staff and reflected in the school's chosen method of organization and management;

(ii)   an explicit commitment by the head and governors to the continuing development of staff members as the major asset available for school improvement, through the preparation and publication of a management development policy incorporated within the school development plan;

(iii)   an acceptance that staff development is a major area of personal accountability for the head even though the administrative functions may be delegated;

(iv)   the establishment of an appropriate management structure which enables new tasks and responsibilities to be undertaken efficiently and allows staff to gain motivation from success;

(v)   recognition that adequate supervision and support for staff in their daily tasks of managing the school is the core element in developing their management performance;

(vi)   integration of procedures for the review and appraisal of individual, team and institutional performance;

(vii)   provision of supporting activities through adjustments to job descriptions and priorities, the resources available to do the job, and the level and quality of routine advice and supervision;

(viii)   access to special learning or training opportunities and peer-group exchange;

(ix)   strategies for succession planning and career development providing new job, task or project opportunities, and induction into these roles;

(x)   support for teachers to review their own experience, to help determine their personal development plans and build portfolios of experience throughout their career.

This list of characteristics effectively maps the goals of school management for staff development. All are important and all are necessary in a comprehensive policy for staff development. If a school can exhibit only some of those characteristics, the resulting staff development is likely to be incomplete also and the benefits to the school will be seriously reduced.

In the management of staff development the role of headteachers is crucial. Their personal styles vary from those who have traditionally provided the school with all its ideas and decisions to others who see themselves as facilitators to a staff working as a team of equals. Those in the first category often find they have to change their position quite radically in order to establish the climate in which staff development can prosper. Initially there can be difficulties with a staff unused to offering ideas or unfamiliar with the strategies of problem-solving. Often they are also unused to working as a team. The heads in turn may feel a loss of control, a frustration at the slowness of progress and a concern that ultimately the outcomes may not match their own preferences. For them, the ideas of the organizational development (O.D.) movement will perhaps be helpful. In essence, its work suggests that in changing the way in which a group works together, the leader should concentrate on the following strategy:

(i)   clarify communication procedures in the school,

(ii)   seek the approval and the commitment of all concerned,

(iii)   work from a basis of fact, not of opinion or emotion,
(iv)   enhance the ways in which the staff work together as a group,
(v)   broaden the base of decision-making within the group,
(vi)   agree a plan for dealing with problem-solving before the problems arise,
(vii) build in plans from the beginning for evaluating progress.

In small schools the head will retain the responsibility for staff development and the problem will be to ensure that the staff themselves share ownership of it. In larger schools there may be a coordinator for staff development or a professional tutor or some similar role. This person needs a clearly defined brief which is fully understood by the staff and which makes clear to everyone what are the respective powers of the head, the coordinator and other people with managerial roles.

Typically, the coordinator's role will encompass some or all of the following:

*   facilitation and coordination of groups charged with needs identification, planning and implementation of staff development;
*   liaison between senior management and staff;
*   distribution of information about staff development opportunities arriving from outside the school;
*   transmission of the school's own needs to external sources of support.

In some cases, schools have set up a staff development group or committee. In their cases, too, clear definition of the committee's role with respect to those of the head and the coordinator, if there is one, is of paramount importance.

Schools involved in the Support for Innovation Project suggested the following arguments for involving a committee of staff in the process:

(i)   the group acts as a 'think tank', generating more ideas than the managers might on their own;
(ii)   it allows ideas to emerge from staff who are not part of the formal management structure, who often feel left out;
(iii) it harnesses the energies of the real leaders of staff opinion, who are not always those in authority;

(iv)   it gets closer to the real concerns of staff;
(v)   for staff, involvement is itself a development activity.

There are, however, some hazards:

(i)   in larger schools there can often be problems of communication between the group and the staff in general;
(ii)   such a group can threaten the traditional power structure in the school and create tensions with heads of department or curriculum coordinators;
(iii) the coordinator may feel divided loyalties between those to the group and those to the management team.

Whatever the structure used to manage staff development in a school, we should never lose sight of the fact that staff development is much more than simply enabling people to extend their knowledge. Changes of behaviour are involved and such changes often require modification of attitudes or values. These are delicate and time-consuming processes. Individuals react positively or negatively according to their own beliefs and earlier experiences, or because of pressures from their colleagues or because of the demands of the particular activity.

The Support for Innovation Project (1989) identified three major types of response from staff members faced with change. The Project categorized them as follows:

(i)   There will be colleagues who naturally accommodate developments. They are likely to have:
    (a)   a successful background in development,
    (b)   been in a supportive environment or team,
    (c)   been involved in a needs identification process,
    (d)   confidence based on their background of experience and are able to take risks.
(ii)   There will be those who, at least initially, will probably be resistant to change. This may be the result of one or more of a range of factors:
    (a)   previous involvement in innovations had not been successful, perhaps because they were not implemented and institutionalized in such a way that significant improvement in children's learning took place;
    (b)   concern arising from the possibility of being made to feel de-skilled, insecure or vulnerable;

(c) there may be a perceived challenge to status;

(d) it is not clear how an appropriate time commitment can be made easily;

(e) the idea runs 'against the grain' of the teacher's own philosophy.

(iii) There will be the majority who remain neutral and uncommitted.

The Project team went on to suggest that the managerial approach to the three groups has to be different; supporting those who are comfortable with change, encouraging those who feel resistant to engage with the problem in an objective way and creating an environment in which the uncommitted are encouraged to participate.

A School Policy for Staff Development

Few schools at present have a clear staff development policy but the lack of movement which currently characterizes the profession, the introduction of school development plans, the development of appraisal and the devolution to schools of funds for INSET all make it a very high priority for the future. A staff development policy statement could take many forms but it is likely to encompass:

* a statement of values, agreed by the staff, concerning the principles underlying staff development, to which they subscribe;

* a statement of more specific objectives for staff development in that school, growing out of the principles;

* an indication of how in practice the school will work with the individual teacher to address those objectives. This might include the consultative and negotiating structures, arrangements for allocating resources, evaluation and monitoring arrangements and role definitions of those involved;

* a statement of entitlement delineating what support any teacher might expect, for example during the induction year, after appraisal, or as a regular INSET entitlement.

Why is it that so many policies lie in cupboards gathering dust after consuming many hours of sweat and tears during their construction? Sometimes it is because the perceived goal of the exercise was limited to getting something on paper to satisfy an external demand or to ward off marauding inspectors. More often it is because the resources necessary to implement the policy have never been committed to it. There are two lessons to be drawn from this observation. The first is that no policy should be agreed without consideration of, and commitment to, the resource implications. The second lesson is to realize that until resources are allocated to a policy that policy doesn't exist, there is simply an aspiration.

The obvious starting point is to allocate a budget for staff development, but this may need to be broken down in some detail to indicate the priorities accorded to the different objectives in the development policy. It will be important to know, for example, how much is available for evaluation of the school's teaching and learning practice, how much for curriculum change and how much for individual career and personal development.

Some of the constraints upon staff development call for more than the allocation of funds if they are to be removed. Timetables can be constructed so as to allow team teaching or support teaching or curriculum group meetings provided the need is established early enough and is given sufficient priority. Small schools, particularly primary schools with teaching heads, have severe limitations upon their room for manoeuvre in timetabling, but if the need is established and given high priority it is often possible to find ways round the problem.

The problem of the effective use of supply cover is a very serious one. As the amount of school-based INSET has increased, it has created two kinds of pressure. The first is that there is not sufficient supply cover to meet the need and the second is that, even when it is available, it disrupts the continuity of learning which is so important to pupils. It also tends to create extra work in preparation for the staff who are to be released. There is no easy solution to this problem. Enhanced staffing ratios have been tried and are helpful, but there are still days when more cover is needed than is available. A more rigorous and earlier planning of INSET needs and provision might improve the planned use of supply staff but the demands of replacement due to illness are still likely to ruin the best-laid plans at a very late stage.

Staff development days have ensured that all schools have a small number of days per year which they can give to staff development, though under the pressure of national initiatives many of these have been taken up with consolidating knowledge of national demands and have not grown from the school's own needs. Nevertheless these days do allow an opportunity to address whole-school issues in a planned way. They are particularly successful if one or more are built into a longer activity, involving classroom work or observation or small group work between meetings. There will always be a tension in teachers' minds between teaching the children and becoming involved in INSET. This can only be resolved if, individually and as a staff, teachers agree on the contribution of INSET to their children's learning and then accord it the appropriate priority. They can then leave their classes without feeling guilty but in the knowledge that what they are learning to do is valuable for their pupils.

The Staff Development Plan

Another reason why staff development policies lie mouldering in cupboards is that schools may have no plan which links policy to action. Such a plan is vital if resources for staff development are to be used in a thought-out way, paying due attention to policy goals and achieving a sensible balance between school needs and individual needs.

There are three sources which feed into a staff development plan:

(i)   the staff development policy,
(ii)   the school development plan, and
(iii)   targets and action points arising from teacher appraisal.

Staff development policy will remain reasonably constant from year to year but school development plans and appraisal action points change every year so there is a point each year when this information must be brought together and reviewed in the light of the policy so as to establish priorities. Some schools do this by means of a staff development committee, in others it is seen as a task for the head, perhaps assisted by the coordinator for staff development if there is one. It is, of course, a crucial step in the whole process and not a comfortable one, for available resources restrict the scope of what is possible to less than that which is desirable. Some things and some people lose out at this stage and it is important to talk to those concerned so that they understand the reasons for the decisions.

Although the pace of change sometimes makes it difficult, it is worth trying to establish a rolling programme, say on a three-year basis, which provides: (i)   the definitive plan for the coming year; (ii)   some major features for the following year — these may be essential developments following on from the first year's commitments or planned new development; (iii)   anticipated features of the third year, mostly those growing out of first and second year commitments. Neither the second or third year plans can be complete because the required information from school planning and appraisal is not yet available, but sketching in what is known helps to create continuity in planning. Even the definitive plan for the first year requires flexibility to be built in, and some resource allocation held back to meet unanticipated needs is a sensible precaution in the plan.

When the plan is put on paper it is good for staff cohesion if the rationale for priorities and choices is spelled out. The rationale may not please everyone but making it available removes speculation and encourages open discussion. In mapping out the plan on paper, some schools start from their staff development policy, demonstrating how each aspect of the policy has been converted into activities. Other schools start from the list of priorities or by describing what is planned for the whole staff, for groups of staff and for individuals. In the latter cases it is essential that at some point the relationship between the plan and the policy is demonstrated.

However the list is organized, it is beneficial to include within it

* the proposed participants,
* the purpose/goal of the activity,
* the type of activity,
* its cost, and
* how the school will use the outcome of the activity.

Managing the Integration of Staff Development with School Development

It is comparatively easy to erect models for staff development, teacher appraisal or school development which are each consistent within themselves, one stage leading logically to another, and which indicate desirable links with the others. We have, for example, discussed a pattern for staff development which contains policy, evaluation, planning and execution. Similarly teacher appraisal has a pattern of data collection, discussion and follow-up, and school development has evaluation, audit, planning and action.

In real life, however, the school has to deal with all three simultaneously, so consideration has to be given to integrating the three processes and to ensuring that the desirable links between them are

Figure 8.1   The Planning Cycle

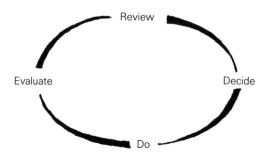

forged at the right time. All three processes are cyclic in form and each follows the pattern described in Figure 8.1, but there can be no certainty that the natural cycle periods will coincide.

How then can the three processes be brought together within an integrated management structure? Even though appraisal runs on a two-year cycle and school development planning partly on a one-year cycle and partly on a longer timescale, it seems sensible to review all three together once a year.

Arising from the school development plan will be school needs which must be recognized in the staff development plan and may need to be considered by appropriate individuals within their appraisal. Arising from teacher appraisal are individual targets which must be incorporated into the staff development plan and may have an influence on the school development plan. Arising from staff development are changes in knowledge and skill which need to be recognized in the school development plan.

It follows that at an early stage of each appraisal, participants should consider whether any newly emerging school needs require their attention. The staff development planning process needs to be fed with a summary of new appraisal targets as well as the new school needs. Later in its cycle, school development planning must take into account new targets arising from appraisal and new capacities which the school now has as a result of staff development. This will allow the school to make active use of the outcomes of staff development, at the same time increasing the motivation of staff because their effort in acquiring the new skills is being recognized by use of them.

In this integrating process, knowledge will always be partial, the question will always be 'What is the latest state of our knowledge?' However, that uncertainty serves to emphasize the dynamic nature of this process. It is a model of constant development.

Figure 8.2   Integrating the Process

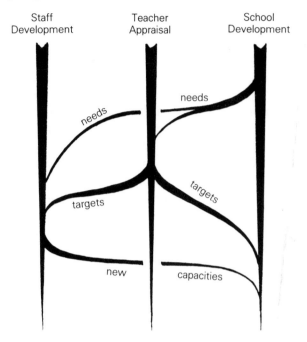

Staff Development Days

Staff development days can be very significant in the development of a school and its staff:

* They bring together the whole staff for a much longer time than is normally possible.
* They are very intensive events which build up a team spirit and a sense of shared achievement.
* They allow a mixture of learning styles — lecture, discussion, experiential learning etc.
* They can be devised as part of a longer developmental programme.

It goes without saying that such intensive activity requires intensive planning if it is to be successful. The impact of one poorly-executed staff development day is as strongly negative as a good one is positive. It is therefore worth paying considerable attention to how staff development days can be used constructively.

(i)   Awareness-raising

At the start of a new development, or at the point where staff are reviewing an area of their practice, a staff 'conference' can be used to raise awareness of the issue and to explore the staff's views and feelings. Outside speakers can be used to present information or case studies of practice elsewhere, data from within the school can be presented to identify the nature of the problem and consultants can be brought in to address issues which emerge. Such awareness-raising conferences can be very powerful weapons. Issues can be pursued in depth and a considerable head of steam can be developed which will drive the development for some time. Teachers can establish owner-ship of the issue and where consensus results this often leads to a major step forward in the school's practice. During the conference teachers get to know one another better and this helps the staff to become more cohesive.

Alongside such advantages there are some dangers. If there has been inadequate preparation of the staff, the zeal of the outsider may be seen as pressure selling and lead to the rejection of the message. The exploration of staff feelings can sometimes emphasize a fun-damental split within the staff to the extent that further progress is impossible.

The messages are, therefore,

* know the staff well;
* plan carefully, produce preparatory materials to guide partici-pants' thinking;
* brief your contributors carefully;
* brief and provide support materials for group leaders;
* think carefully about how to bring together individual opin-ion or feedback from group discussion in a positive way;
* consider how afterwards you will approach this issue with people who missed the day, or who dissented from the gener-al view.

(ii)   Review and Development

Sometimes it is best to begin a development by undertaking some small-scale research into school practice, or to try something new in an experimental way. In such instances, it is often very helpful to dedicate a staff development day to reviewing the evidence or progress so far, exploring what it means and deciding what steps to take next. On the whole, these days present fewer problems in terms of establishing the right climate as the preparatory work will have prepared the staff for it. The process of analysis and decision-making will call for careful consideration as it is essential to arrive at decisions about the next steps and that those steps should be practical. It is vital to avoid rushed conclusions which cannot be realized afterwards, though equally a decision to 'leave it until our next meeting' loses valuable momentum.

(iii)   Dissemination

When a group of staff members has done some development work or some planning for the school it is often useful to use a staff development day to inform and train their colleagues. This is frequently a highly successful activity if the teachers outside the group contributed to setting the brief for the group, have been kept informed of its progress and feel the group has been doing the work for them. There have been some notable failures in cases where some of these precepts have been ignored. If teachers feel this is a management ploy to enforce an unwelcome change, it will not be successful. Equally, if the function of the day is perceived to be to press the interests of one group of staff upon the rest, there are often difficulties.

In the last few years, small schools have increasingly joined 'clusters' or 'consortia' for INSET purposes. When they have staff development days together there are added difficulties in ensuring that the needs of each school are going to be met by the day. However, if this condition is met, there are many advantages — schools are able to share good practice, teachers are reassured to find other people share their problems, networks of advice and support are strengthened, and follow-up activities involving staff in each of the schools can be built in.

However staff development days are organized, attention must be paid to what happens when they are over. A written report of outcomes, agreements and decisions is essential for memories are short! Because staff development days are outside the school's normal decision-making procedures, it is worth making sure that its outcomes have been incorporated into the normal procedures, for example the allocation of INSET funds or the ordering of school materials or equipment.

The Support for Innovation Project asked schools to identify planning factors which contributed to the success of a staff day. Example 8.3 gives one school's reply, which contains much good advice.

Example 8.3   Factors which Contributed to the Success of a Staff Day

1. The timing just happened to be perfect. Collaborative projects were at delicate stages: there was a climate of sharing and reflecting in the school. The end of March was a suitable time given the need for follow-up work. The long summer term allowed for this.
2. We decided that this was to be a staff conference and as such it should be planned and led by the staff. There were to be no outside speakers. A 'GRIDS' style questionnaire was sent out to all staff listing five major curricular and pastoral developments in the school. Teachers were asked to state preference for topics they would like to work on or to suggest other areas we might have missed. The decision to use current staff expertise was an important element in the creation of a corporate staff identity.
3. Long hours were spent planning the event, down to the last detail. Two colleagues were despatched to check out hotel arrangements and sample the hospitality! Activities were drawn up, tried out by a sample group and often scrapped. We looked again at timings of activities, the balance of work, group sizes, whole staff participation, and above all the credibility of what we were trying to do. We refined and refined our programmes, the senior staff as a team looking critically at all ideas offered.
4. Each group had joint leadership, and a number of presentations were made by staff in teams. In this way members of staff were given a role to play in the Conference.
5. We produced a sixty page booklet, printed as professionally as possible, containing full details of the agenda, articles by staff, notes of recent meetings, copies of relevant articles from the press and education reference books. We managed to issue the booklet a full week before the Conference to allow time for reading, thinking and discussion.
6. Our school secretary attended the weekend and took full notes and tape recordings; all the points were documented in a Conference Report.

Source: Support for Innovation Project (1989) *Thinking Schools*, Cambridge, Cambridge Institute of Education.

Evaluating Staff Development

If staff development is to become a much more significant part of the life of a school and to take more of its resources, it is inevitable and desirable that it should be evaluated. At the school level, it is worth distinguishing two different areas for evaluation, INSET activities and the school's programme of staff development as a whole.

Evaluating INSET Activities

There have been considerable developments in evaluating some aspects of INSET activities. Any substantial activity now has its end-of-activity questionnaire. The simple ones unfortunately produce simple answers, usually restricted to immediate participant satisfaction — 'did you like it?' rather than 'has it made any change in your

practice?' Such evidence should not be neglected, for dissatisfied participants are unlikely to volunteer for more, but as a basis for planning
future developments it is not enough. A fuller evaluation needs to
examine

* participant satisfaction,
* impact on teachers' attitudes,
* impact on teachers' performance,
* impact on practice in the school.

Figure 8.4 lists some of the evaluation strategies available to us.

Evaluation by correspondence is relatively quick and can cover
large numbers of people. It gives quite good indications of participant
satisfaction, though detailed questionnaires which invite item-by-item
criticism need a complementary section on general response to the
activity if balance is to be maintained. These approaches do not tell us
about impact on performance or school practice though they can elicit

Figure 8.4   Evaluation Strategies

Evaluation Strategies

A.   *By correspondence*

1. tick-in-box questionnaire
2. structured free-response questionnaire
3. open-ended essay-type questionnaire
4. letters before and after:
   'tell me your hopes and expectations of the course and your pressing concerns at school'
   'this is what you said before the course; would you now comment on it in the light of the course?'
5. keeping a diary

B.   *Face to face*

6. interview after — structured or unstructured
7. interview before and after
8. interview at regular intervals before, during and after

C.   *By participation*

9. participant observer

D.   *By objective measures*

10. measures of attitude change
11. teacher performance indicators
12. pupil performance indicators

some opinions about changes in attitude. We have to be careful, however, not to confuse opinion with fact. Several studies have shown us that the perceptions of individuals are not borne out by colleagues or pupils. The structured free-response questionnaire is quite good at exploring attitudes and the before-and-after letter is particularly good at highlighting changes which retrospective questionnaires miss because teachers have forgotten where they started. An evaluation diary, completed as the INSET activity proceeds, helps us to understand the teacher's own processes but is difficult to summarize or generalize.

Interviewing can give us deeper knowledge of attitudes, as it allows us to probe, to follow-up and to check our perceptions with the responder in a way that questionnaires cannot. However, it is a costly procedure in terms of time and is likely to be done only on a sampling basis and for very important issues. A participant observer, who takes part in the whole process as a participant but looks at it through the eyes of an evaluator, is a useful alternative. This is particularly so if the observer has time to talk to other participants about their perceptions.

Only objective measures can really take us confidently into the impact on teacher behaviour and school practice. Changes in teacher performance can be sought through classroom observation or task observation as indeed can the impact on practice in the school. Sometimes other teachers and the headteacher can offer information which helps to establish whether changes have taken place. Documentary evidence, such as schemes of work or pupils' work, can also provide useful evidence. Collecting data of this kind is clearly time-consuming. It may also have to continue over a considerable period for effects of this kind may not be observable immediately. It is clear that in future more evidence about performance is going to be needed and it may be necessary to consider whether schools should establish routine data-gathering procedures which would facilitate all the planning processes and incidentally provide evidence about the effectiveness of INSET.

Evaluating Staff Development Programmes

When we switch the focus from evaluating the INSET activity to evaluating the whole programme of staff development the field broadens enormously. Judy Bradley (1983), examining staff development schemes in further education, describes implementation criteria and impact criteria which are immediately applicable to our considerations. The implementation criteria she identified were:

* Have definite targets been set for the various areas covered by the aims and objectives of the scheme?
* What are these and by what stage should they be met?
* Have these been discussed with members of staff directly involved?
* Have their suggestions been incorporated?
* What kinds of information are being collected in order to establish that targets are being reached?
* What kinds of information are being collected to ensure that procedures are adequate, e.g. on methods of application, financial considerations, channels of communication?
* What are the greatest barriers to implementation, e.g. facilities, resources, channels of communication, interpersonal relations?
* What steps have been taken in an attempt to overcome these difficulties?

She went on to identify both direct and indirect criteria for impact:

Direct effects
* Were programme objectives met for the last academic year?
* What factors helped or hindered the achievement of objectives?
* Has the level of activity and support increased?
* Have communication links been established or improved?
* Have previously identified needs been significantly met? In which areas?
* What college or individual needs still have not been met?
* What changes in teaching or management practice have been noted?
* How were these identified, e.g. by student rating, observation, assessment by peers?
* Is there any evidence of impact on student performance? How was this obtained?

Indirect effects
* How have actual and unanticipated outcomes differed?
* What unanticipated benefits (e.g. collaboration) or negative outcomes (e.g. alienation) has the scheme generated?

Figure 8.5   Checklist for Evaluating Staff Development

Checklist for Evaluating Staff Development

Preparation

Was the process of identification of need accurate? Was there consensus about the needs among all the people concerned?
Did the school do the necessary preparatory work

- (i)   to enable the teachers taking part to obtain maximum benefit,
- (ii)   to enable other staff to benefit from their experience?

Planning the Activities

Did those who planned the activities have skills in the design of INSET activities?

Were the goals for each activity clearly defined? When change in attitude, teaching style or other fundamental factor was desired, was this made clear or was it hidden behind a facade of content allowing participants to miss the point of the exercise? Were the goals shared by the participants in the activity?

Was the methodology appropriate to the goals? Was it appropriate for adult learners?

Execution of Activities

Did the participants recognize the purpose and value of constituent parts of the activities?

Did the participants in fact share common purposes and goals or were there 'hidden curricula' which impeded group coherence?

Did the participants enjoy the process?

Did they find it of value to themselves professionally?

Did they feel it equipped them to help their colleagues?

Impact

Was the school willing to change?

Did the school make use of the participants' experience?

Did the INSET activity result in a change?

Was the change effective and in line with the needs and the priorities of the school?

Figure 8.5 shows a checklist which has been used in schools to aid the evaluation of staff development. There is again benefit in undertaking this kind of evaluation as an integral part of the school's planning procedures, rather than regarding it as a 'bolt-on extra'. There is a growing recognition that evaluation is not a peripheral activity but one that is central to further development.

The Way Ahead

Staff development is a complex activity which cannot be left to change; it must be managed and managed well.

The School Management Task Force Report summarizes the actions required from schools as follows:

* Prepare and publish a school management development policy incorporated within the school development plan, which recognizes that staff development is a major area of personal accountability for the head;
* establish appropriate management structures to reflect new tasks and responsibilities;
* provide adequate supervision and support for staff in their daily tasks;
* establish integrated procedures for the review and appraisal of individual, team and institutional performance;
* support each teacher in reviewing experience throughout his or her career;
* promote strategies for succession planning and career development that provide preparation for and induction to new posts, and new task, job or project opportunities.

In managing staff development the emphasis should be on continuous improvement, building upon an established base. Revolution may occasionally be necessary but it needs a very special kind of aftercare. In most schools, staff development requires an open, supportive climate and participative management and decision-making. These do not fit well with revolutions.

Continuous improvement should not, however, be a passive process. To enable it to succeed schools need to develop:

* a clear, shared policy for staff development;
* a practical staff development plan that clearly links policy with activities;
* a strategy for linking appraisal action points with the staff development plan;
* a method of ensuring that the knowledge and skills gained through staff development are utilized in school development.

Our goal is to interrelate staff development and school development so that they carry each other forward, to the benefit of teachers, school and pupils.

References

BRADLEY, J. (1983) Evaluating staff development schemes, *Educational Research*, Vol. 25, No. 2, June 1983.

DEPARTMENT OF EDUCATION AND SCIENCE (1990) *Developing School Management — The Way Forward*, a report by the School Management Task Force. London, HMSO.

SUPPORT FOR INNOVATION PROJECT (1989) *Thinking Schools*, Cambridge, Cambridge Institute of Education.

Index